CENTENNIAL CITY
Calgary 1894–1994

CALGARY
100
1894 ♦ 1994

New Nouvelles
ALTITUDES
Learned Societies Conference
Congrès des sociétés savantes
THE UNIVERSITY OF CALGARY
June 3 to 18 • 1994 • du 3 au 18 juin

© 1994 The University of Calgary

Canadian Cataloguing in Publication Data

Main entry under title:
Centennial City

Includes bibliographical references.
ISBN 1-895176-57-3

1. Calgary (Alta.) – History. 2. Calgary (Alta.) – Social conditions.
I. Smith, Donald B., 1946-
FC3697.4.C46 1994   971.23'38   C94-910388-8
F1079.5.C35C46 1994

∞ This book is printed on acid-free paper.

A word about the cover:

The historic photograph shows a view of Calgary from the North Hill, around 1890. The spire of the Anglican Church of the Redeemer can be seen in the centre (Glenbow Archives/NA-431-3). The Calgary Sun generously supplied the outline of the modern city skyline. Cliff Kadatz of The University of Calgary's Department of Communications/Media designed the cover and the book.

Table of Contents

The year 1994 is a very special one for Calgarians as it represents our Centennial of incorporation as a city. The year-long celebrations will take their root in the very communities that have both grown up with Calgary and will become an integral part of its future. In many ways, it is a celebration for which we have already spent 100 years preparing.

The City of Calgary is deeply appreciative of its strong cordial relationship with The University of Calgary. As a central institution within our community we are aware that the presence of the University brings us many benefits and strengthens our community. It is not without significance that in the same year we celebrate our Centennial, the city and university have been selected to host the 1994 Learned Societies Conference. We welcome the thousands of delegates to our city and embrace the opportunity to demonstrate our famous western hospitality to visitors from across Canada and around the world.

On behalf of my colleagues on City Council and the citizens of Calgary, I am pleased to recommend to you this book which includes contributions from community and university authors. We hope it will help you to understand more of Calgary's history and some of the things that make Calgary unique.

The citizens of Calgary have planned a full range of activities to commemorate our 100th anniversary as a city. We hope you will enjoy this book as one of the many ways in which all of us can partake in the spirit of this special year.

Sincerely,

Al Duerr
Mayor, the City of Calgary

The University of Calgary salutes The City of Calgary on its Centennial!

We in the University are proud of our close association with our City. It was only through the will and dedicated efforts of Calgarians over many decades that this University came into existence. Continuation of this community support has been instrumental to enabling the University to grow and flourish.

A great proportion of our students are from the City and area. More than 35,000 of our alumni live here, and many participate actively in the life of the community, as do numerous faculty and staff members. We are also one of Calgary's largest employers, and contribute substantially to the local economy. Citizens of Calgary from many walks of life are involved in governance and advisory roles touching virtually every University program. This level and quality of City-University interaction is second to none in the country.

For all of the foregoing reasons, it is with great pleasure that we in the University join with The City of Calgary in celebrating its 100th Anniversary in a special way.

1994 is a distinctive year for the University as we are honoured to host the Learned Societies Conference. Thousands of delegates and guests will come to Calgary to share in the meetings of well over 100 professional and scholarly societies. This unique and prestigious event is serving as the occasion for a City-wide Celebration of Learning, in which all are invited to participate.

The combination of the Learned Societies Conference and the City's Centennial in 1994 provided the occasion for this commemorative book, which includes contributions from both campus and community authors. The generous support of The Calgary Sun and Canada Safeway Limited helped make this book a reality, for which the University is most grateful.

Murray Fraser
President, The University of Calgary

Acknowledgements

Many individuals in the community and at the university contributed to this official centennial project. A special thank you is due to all those who wrote articles, completed the Calgary bibliography, and compiled the historic timeline. Lynette Walton, photo archivist at the Glenbow Archives, located the illustrations from the Glenbow which appear in the text. Joy Bowes and Joyce Woods of the Department of History of The University of Calgary prepared the disk with the final texts, which John King and Shirley Onn then arranged for publication by the University of Calgary Press. Cliff Kadatz of the Department of Communications/Media at the university designed the book.

We very warmly thank our corporate sponsors, The Calgary Sun and Canada Safeway Limited, who, from the outset, supported the idea of writing a commemorative book to mark both Calgary's 100th anniversary, and the holding of the Learned Societies Conference at The University of Calgary. Marcel Clouthier, Kathy Dilts, Randy Hill, Paul Jackson, Craig Martin, Bob Poole, Michele McDonald, Alice Ritchie, and Cheryl Sundell of the Sun all assisted.

Canada Safeway Limited generously provided the grant to pay the book's production costs, making this university and community project possible. With their interest in education and public awareness of our heritage, they have also underwritten the cost of providing two copies of *Centennial City: Calgary 1894-1994* to every school in the Calgary area. We appreciate their assistance in helping us to produce this tribute to our city on its one hundredth anniversary.

Don Smith

An early Safeway store in Calgary, located on the north side of 8th Avenue SE between 1st Street SE and Macleod Trail, now the site of the Olympic Plaza, where the medal presentation ceremonies were held during the 1988 Winter Olympics. Canada Safeway Limited.

Onward! Calgary in the 1890s

Donald Smith and Henry Klassen

The City of Calgary was born amidst a drastic depression, but that did not daunt the man soon to become its first mayor, Wesley Orr. On Christmas Day, 1893, he had written to his daughter, Adelaide, that for the community's motto he would choose "the plain English word, 'Onward'."[1] Worried residents certainly hoped Orr's enthusiasm would soon become a reality.

Only a few years earlier, optimistic perceptions of Calgary's future had prevailed. In 1882, for example, Richard Hardisty of the Hudson's Bay Company commented: "People are flocking in, in connection with the Canadian Pacific Railway and cattle ranches, besides others going in for the purpose of settling down on farms."[2] Writing in 1890, Hudson's Bay Company officer Harrison J. Young claimed that after the CPR's arrival in 1883 Calgary had advanced from "a frontier village" to a "modern town." The "requirements of the people of Calgary today," he added, "are similar to those of

Calgary's Stephen (8th) Avenue, January 23, 1892. The street was named after George Stephen, the first president of the Canadian Pacific Railway. Glenbow Archives/NA-1702-7.

1

Winnipeg and other large cities."[3] But in 1895 Mounted Police Sergeant A.F.M. Brooke's assessment struck a different note: "The population of Calgary is 3,207, which is correct . . . In 1891 there was hardly a vacant house in Calgary, or in the district, and now most of the farmers have left, and gone north, and there are at least fifty vacant houses in town at present."[4]

The town, which became a city in 1894, extended out haphazardly along the CPR line. Amidst false-fronted stores and unkempt vacant lots the few elegant sandstone buildings seemed strangely out of place. The board sidewalks heaved and teetered, only to end in a final step onto a dirt road. Above all, the absence of trees gave the city its non-descript appearance.

Particularly in the summer distinctive odours filled the air. Strong aromas came from the numerous livery stables. The smells of the stables permeated entire city blocks. A stench also arose from the city's cesspools and outdoor privies. Truly the city was in the midst of an envi-

An excursion on the north side of the Bow River, north of St. George's Island, early 1900s. Glenbow Archives/NA-1126-5.

ronmental crisis. A flood of wastes from downtown buildings emptied into an inadequate sewer system, sometimes into downtown cesspools or open street drains. The well for the newly constructed Central School stood close to open outdoor privies.

Yet, one could easily escape to the fresh air of the open countryside. The prairies stood on one side of the city, the foothills on the other. Clearly the city had potential as a place to live and work. The city's centre stood safe from floods on the high ground, half a mile south of the Bow River (although flooding did remain a problem on the lower ground near the river). The Elbow River system provided an ample supply of water, while the Bow River had considerable potential for the development of an irrigation project to open up thousands of acres to cultivation. Most important, the city lay in the centre of ranching and farming country.

Walking was a common pastime. Susie Harris, a teenager in Calgary in the 1890s, treasured the summer beauty of the area north of the townsite. Just beyond the Langevin Bridge (built across the Bow in 1890 by the federal government) the hills lay all bare, until the wild flowers bloomed, "I remember one hill yellow with golden violets, another hill a mass of blue blossoms, and nearby would be a valley red with tiger lilies, and above a blue sky with white floating clouds—and westward always the snowcapped Rocky Mountains."[5]

The stagnant economy after 1891 particularly hurt Calgary's working class. An unskilled labourer lucky enough to find enough regular work, earned only about $35 every month. Fortunately bread was only 2 cents a loaf, and beef cost just 8 cents a pound. A tradesperson might make between $50 and $60. But most work was seasonal and very difficult to obtain in winter. This made the jobs of the small number of permanent municipal employees look very attractive indeed. They earned between $45 and $70 every month. When the town advertised a teaching post in 1892, nearly fifty people applied.

Irregular incomes meant inadequate living quarters. Crowded, cold, and cheaply built dwellings characterized the working poor's accommodation. To make ends meet, bartering became common; landlords sometimes accepted laundry in lieu of rent. The churches acted as best they could as relief agencies, providing temporary support. The benefit societies such as the Masons, Oddfellows, and Foresters came forward to help their members' families.

The City Council showed itself most reluctant to become involved in relief, preferring to leave it to private organizations. On the other hand, anxious to attract industry, it generously provided incentives like a free land site, a cash bonus, and extended tax ex-emption to any "prospective manufactory." The Council believed its mandate to be the promotion of economic growth, not the provision of services. Subsequently, throughout the 1890s, it tolerated the inefficient privately owned water and electric companies and made no effort to establish a municipally owned utilities and waterworks service.

The depression, as well as the city's unsanitary conditions, contributed to problems of public health. On account of the high cost of the pure water that the privately owned waterworks supplied, over half of the city's residents drank partially polluted water from their own wells, some of which were located no further than fifteen feet from their own outhouses.[6] These people depended on outdoor privies and cesspools, as they could not afford to connect their homes with the city's sewerage systems, which in any event did not extend to all parts of the city. Because of its lack of proper sanitation, the city swarmed with house flies (and bed bugs).

In 1895 Calgary officially opened its first modern hospital, built just north of the present Stampede Grounds. The General Hospital's origins can be traced back to a gift of $600 from an elderly Chinese citizen, known in English as Jimmy Smith. Before his death from tuberculosis, he left $600 to be given to a fund to build a public hospital. Jean Drever Pinkham of the Women's Hospital Aid Society led the campaign to establish first a temporary or cottage hospital in 1890, and finally the first permanent structure in 1895.

In choosing the site, the Council showed more interest in its real estate potential, than in its advantages as a location for the sick. Those owning property in East Calgary had the most influence, hence they won the contest. The Council overlooked the importance of a high and dry location, a site with good drainage and good water, one free of excessive noise, and instead placed the hospital between the soap factory and the railroad tracks, in a low-lying area.

The rapid expansion of Calgary in the mid- and late 1880s had led to a scramble for land. The population of the settlement had jumped after the CPR's arrival in 1883, from several hundred to approximately 1,000 by 1885, 2,000 by 1889, and nearly 4,000 by 1891. In the early 1890s, the town's central area occupied about one square mile: Drinkwater Street (2nd Street E.) on the east to Ross Street (4th Street W.) on the west, and north to Angus Avenue (6th Avenue) and south to Van Horne (12th Avenue)—until the city in 1904 introduced numbers for the streets, they bore the names of individuals, mostly the names of CPR officials. In addition to the development around the CPR station, the original core of settlement remained on the east bank of the Elbow, opposite Fort Calgary.

When the value of choice property in the business district shot up from $500 a lot to $2,500, speculators had made small fortunes. The town thus obtained its first moneyed class. They built large houses, a few having five or six bedrooms, a library, sun parlour and billiard room, as well as several huge stone fireplaces. As Senator James Lougheed's house went up, the Calgary Herald gave weekly reports on its construction. The grounds of some residences occupied several lots, and the mansions themselves cost as much as $20,000. Class distinctions descended upon the tiny settlement when those living in the more comfortable houses began calling themselves the better class of people.

A view of Calgary from the east, with the General Hospital shown at the bottom right, 1895. Glenbow Archives/NA-615-1.

Yet, the prosperous and the low-income people still lived side by side. No exclusive neighbourhoods existed. Like other Calgary homes, the mansions looked out on plank sidewalks, dusty unpaved streets, and occasionally a stray cow. Prosperous families, small wage earners, and the poor intermingled, as their homes stood on the same streets and often on the same blocks. The city's "elite" wanted their homes close to their business or place of work. Only

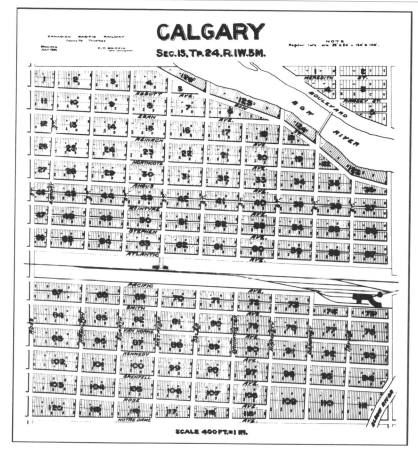

CALGARY

SEC. 15, TR. 24, R. 1 W. 5 M.

This map prepared in 1902 shows the city's street names before 1904. The CPR station, for instance, was located at the junction of McTavish (Centre) Street and Atlantic (9th) Avenue.

in the early twentieth century did the well-to-do acquire an option. Streetcars and the automobile, which arrived in numbers in the 1910s, contributed to the movement of middle-class citizens to suburbs like Elbow Park.

At the turn of the century, Calgarians of all classes faced two great challenges: flooding and fire.

Unusual spring run-offs and rainstorms frequently led to the inundation of low-lying areas. In June 1897, a flood rushed through the city at ten o'clock one evening. It wrecked two of the city's three bridges. All that you could see of Prince's Island in the middle of the Bow was the tops of the trees.

Fire remained a constant danger. The big fire of November 1886 destroyed sixteen of the tiny community's best buildings. After that disaster the town began to use local sandstone for almost all of its important structures. They had to do this in order to obtain lower fire insurance rates. Soft and easily carved when quarried, sandstone turned hard with age. Immigrant Scottish stone masons used the rock to transform Calgary's principal buildings from frame to fire-proof stone.

Calgary in the 1890s was a British Canadian town. According to the census of 1901, slightly over 80 percent of the residents were of direct British descent. The only substantial minorities were the Germans and Scandinavians (at 5 percent each) and those of French background (3 percent). Asians numbered only 64 out of the 4,400 people in the city, and Native people only 100. Most of Calgary's business and social leaders were born in eastern Canada, men like William Pearce, James Lougheed, Pat Burns, and James Walker from Ontario, and A.E. Cross, Charles Rouleau, Peter Prince, and Wesley Orr from Quebec. Some, however, like William Roper Hull, George Clift King, and Thomas Underhill were English. Two of the leading women in the community did come from Western Canada: Belle Hardisty Lougheed, born at Fort Resolution on Great Slave Lake, and Jean Drever Pinkham, born in Red River. Jane Howse Livingston and Adelaide Belcourt Glenn, the Metis wives of the area's two original settlers, Sam Livingston and John Glenn, were from Alberta. Men outnumbered women by nearly two to one in the 1890s.

Parents looked to the local public and separate schools to teach their children the foundations of British citizenship. Students of all economic backgrounds attended the Calgary public schools, the Sacred Heart Convent, and the Lacombe Separate School. Here, in large, crowded, poorly ventilated classrooms, their sons and daughters learned

Sunday skating party on the Elbow River. Glenbow Archives/NA-5374-1.

poems and stories in the Ontario Readers, sang songs like "Soldiers of the Queen" and "Rule Britannia," read English literature, and studied the political history of Britain and Canada. In the 1890s, Lillian Costello, the first non-Native girl born in Calgary (December 16, 1883), worked her way through the school system. Her father, Irish-born John Costello, was the first school teacher in Calgary.

Calgary teachers divided their classes with an average number of fifty pupils into two sections: the girls on one side and the boys on the other. James Short, principal of Central School from 1888 to 1892, and the teacher of the first high school class in Calgary, later recalled: "The boys all wore cowboy hats and knew all about the diamond hitch and bronco busting."[7] Attendance could have been better, one class in 1892 had eighty-eight students on the rosters but an average attendance of twenty-seven. Daily attendance in the 1890s averaged about fifty percent.

In the 1890s, Calgarians had opportunities for fun: walking along the riverbanks, skating in winter on the frozen streams, playing cricket or baseball in the summer, going hunting and fishing. From the town's beginning, horse racing was immensely popular. Citizens bet heavily on footraces, which involved invited professionals or local runners like the phenomenal Deerfoot, the celebrated Blackfoot Indian runner. Some touring companies brought music and theater to the city; local amateurs themselves put on concerts, plays, and even operas. Cards parties in homes were popular.

The town also looked outward. As early as 1885, the sandstone operators at the Shaganappi Point quarry had discovered a market for their sandstone for use in erecting public buildings in Regina. To enlarge his horizons, Daniel Webster Marsh, a Calgary merchant and former mayor, visited the World's Columbian Exposition in Chicago in 1893. Like Marsh, Donald McLean of the Alberta Roller Mills in Calgary also travelled to Chicago and there won a medal for his fine flour at the Exposition.

Only a handful of people in the 1890s had roots in the community extending back to its origins. The newcomers knew little about its founding in 1875. When Ephrem Brisebois, the settlement's founder, died on February 13, 1890, in Minnedosa, Manitoba, neither of the two papers, the Calgary Herald and the Calgary Tribune, carried his obituary. Only fifteen years earlier, the French-Canadian NWMP officer had founded "Fort Brisebois," just a few months later to become "Fort Calgary" on the suggestion of Colo-

nel James Macleod, the man soon to be named the new NWMP Commissioner. After Brisebois had left in 1876, Calgary forgot him.

Calgarians, however, did remember and honour Colonel Macleod, who, after his resignation from the force in 1880 had become a respected magistrate in the District of Alberta. Just several months before his death on September 5, 1894, he had taken up residence in the city he had named after a favourite spot on the Isle of Mull on the west coast of his native Scotland. The funeral procession on September 7th proceeded from the judge's sandstone house by the Bow River, down Stephen (8th) Avenue to the Anglican Church of the Redeemer. Many could not obtain standing room within the church, so great was the crowd.[8]

One man who harkened back to the period before the NWMP's arrival was the District of Alberta's first and sole M.P. in the House of Commons in Ottawa from 1887 to 1896. An American from Vermont and a U.S. Army veteran, D.W. Davis, entered the Canadian West as a whisky trader but, like many of his colleagues, had quickly switched to legitimate business once Colonel Macleod and the NWMP came west in 1874. The Mounties had even asked him, as the agent for I.G. Baker & Co., to build "Fort Brisebois" for them. Under his supervision, the Metis did, putting up the upright posts, chinking them with mud, and adding a mud roof to protect—yes—the mud floors.

In an age of strong investigative reporting, Davis might well have been exposed as the Indian-killer he was. In a letter written home from Fort Whoop-Up, just a year before the Mounties came west, he had mentioned the two murders. "My work is not without

Sarcee dance on McTavish (Centre) Street, 1889, marking the turning on of Calgary's street lights. Glenbow Archives/NA-1004-1.

danger as it is trading with Indians altho I have never been hurt or scared yet had to kill 2 last winter on act [account] of stealing horses that is the only trouble I ever had with them."[9]

In the 1890s, Calgarians frequently saw Indians in the city, in family groups, the man riding first, then the woman with the travois, a child or two riding with her and perhaps another on the travois. Then came a string of ponies, which they sold, and always at least one Indian dog. Boys bargained for the cayuses, the usual price being $2. This certainly beat the cost of a bicycle, which sold until the late 1890s for between $75 and $100.

In the 1890s, Calgarians knew the sound of Native drumming. "The Indians," Susie Harris recalled years later, "used to hold pow-wows in a vacant block near the station. The solemn beating of their tom toms, a weird sound, made the shivers run down my back."

The Harris family lived in a brown bungalow on MacTavish (now Centre Street). On the north side of the river stood the shack of a Metis named Larondel. Another Metis used to regale the Harris children "with tales about driving the buffalo over the cut bank which towered above the river." The last buffalo herds had vanished from southern Alberta in 1879.

The presence of a permanent force of a hundred well-disciplined Mounties helped to maintain order in Calgary. When a drunken mob attacked the Chinese community in 1892, the NWMP intervened and stopped the looting. They allowed the frightened Chinese to sleep in the police barracks. The mob had held the Chinese responsible for an outbreak of smallpox. The epidemic resulted in three deaths.

Calgary's image as an unruly, riotous community worried business and civic leaders. After the troubles of 1892, NWMP Inspector Ross Cuthbert wrote: "It is difficult to determine how the whole thing will end. The feeling is bitter between sections of the town. The respectable portion with a majority of the town council are for law and order. The remainder under the mayor [Alexander Lucas] are in favour of letting the mob have its way and no police protection. There is no doubt that at the present time should it become known that the Mounted Police would not interfere, life and property in Calgary would be at the mercy of a drunken mob."[10] To Cuthbert and many other Calgarians, the mob action and the anti-Chinese feeling undermined the open, friendly atmosphere and generous western hospitality that made Calgary a place of opportunity.

That same year, 1892, the Territorial Government in Regina had ended the law that prohibited the sale of liquor in the Northwest Territories. (Alberta and Saskatchewan were created out of the Northwest Territories in 1905.) It had proved impossible to enforce. NWMP Superintendent J.H. McIllree reported as much in 1890: "At present, I believe liquor is more plentiful and cheaper in this District than it has been for a long time. . . . It is almost an impossibility to get a case [against anyone] of selling intoxicants. Neither a policeman or a civilian will inform except in isolated cases as owing to the general feeling against the liquor law. It means social ostracism to the informer."[11]

Moral crimes were not as vigorously prosecuted as civic disturbances. The Mounties did launch raids on brothels, but usually contented themselves with the imposition of fines on those convicted or issued warnings to leave town or face jail.

Calgary had a suspected abortionist in the early 1890s, a Robert Campbell, known by his nickname of "Dr. Lovingheart." In May 1894, the local Calgary police arrested him—charging him with practising medicine without a licence. He paid his fine of $25 on his conviction. Several months later he was charged with attempting to procure an abortion. Although the judge threw the case out, Dr. Lovingheart at this point left Calgary forever.[12]

When the City of Calgary came into existence on January 1, 1894, political power rested in the hands of a small business and professional elite. High property qualifications and public apathy enabled this group to control local politics. Almost all members of the town and city councils in the late nineteenth century were merchants.

Preoccupied by the necessity of making a living, the electorate left the task of governing to those males with some capital who had the benefit of a good education. Women were not eligible for office. While wives of ratepayers could vote in territorial elections,

Calgary's first City Council, January 1, 1894. The man to be elected on January 15, 1894, as the city's first mayor, Wesley Orr, appears standing on the extreme right. Glenbow Archives/NA-1402-1.

the city of Calgary denied them the vote in municipal elections. The prevailing male attitude held that women's most important function was to marry and bear children.

Easily the most powerful figure in local government from 1888 to 1897 was Wesley Orr, the city's first mayor. He worked single-mindedly to build a southeastern industrial base for Calgary, where he and other council members had substantial properties. Calgary's business community had convinced many others that their interests and those of the city itself coincided.

Born in Quebec in 1831, Orr had left home at age twenty-three to seek his fortune. In both Ontario and the United States, he worked at many occupations, including cattle-dealer, sales representative, manufacturer, teacher, storekeeper, and lumber agent. Yet success always eluded him. Advised in 1883 of the investment possibilities of Fort Calgary, he and an associate spent $10,000 to purchase the sure site, a quarter section south of the Bow River and east of the Elbow River, opposite Fort Calgary. Orr invested all of his money in the venture only to see the CPR select as the townsite a location one mile farther west. To promote the commercial value of his lands, Orr moved west and soon entered civic politics. His wife Priscilla refused to follow him west. He settled in Calgary in 1886 as a single parent with his seven-year-old son.

At an age when most men begin to slow down, Orr, in his late fifties and early sixties, speeded up. He operated a stone quarry, sold real estate, traded in buffalo bones, and worked as a financial agent. From 1888 to 1890 and from 1892 to 1893, he sat on the town council, chairing the committee of public works. In effect, he became a full-time civic official. He worked for the establishment of Calgary's privately owned electric light, water, and sewage systems, as well as for the incorporation of Calgary, January 1, 1894. He worked for the promotion of irrigation. He had a vision of a prosperous Calgary, lifted out of its depression. Elected mayor on January 15th, Orr gave his best to improve his personal fortunes and the city's.

In spite of his commitment and unswerving faith in the city's future, Wesley Orr did not live to see it. His health failed during his second tenure as mayor in 1897. Calgary's great champion died on February 1898, only a few years before the land boom of 1901 to 1911 raised Calgary's population tenfold from 4,400 to over 44,000, which would confirm all his predictions. The motto which he chose for his adopted city reminds us of his philosophy: *Onward.*[13]

Notes

The authors thank David Bright, Uta Fox, and Mark Ogilvie, for information contributed to the writing of this article, and particularly Max Foran for his comments on it, as well as for background on Wesley Orr. Our thanks to Paul Jackson, Editor of the Calgary Sun, for his suggestions after reading a draft of the article.

[1] Wesley F. Orr to Mrs. Addie C. Wood, London, Ontario, dated Calgary, Christmas Dec. 1893, Wesley F. Orr Papers, Glenbow Archives. Orr named a short street in east Calgary, in the tract he controlled, after her. The street named after his son Lorne disappeared some years ago, but Adelaide Street still remains, just south of 9th Avenue SE. It joins 8th Street SE.

[2] Richard Hardisty to J.A. Grahame, dated Edmonton, June 20, 1882, Provincial Archives of Manitoba, Hudson's Bay Company Archives, D 20/23, folio 161d.

[3] Provincial Archives of Manitoba, Hudson's Bay Company Archives, D 20/62, folio 212, Edmonton, August 22, 1890, Harrison J. Young to Joseph Wrigley.

[4] A.F.M. Brooke to Z.T. Wood, dated Calgary, June 14, 1895, National Archives of Canada, RG 18, Royal Canadian Mounted Police Records, vol. 370, file 179-1895.

[5] This and other quotes by Susie Harris Knight appear in her memoir, in the Glenbow Archives, acquired February 27, 1973.

[6] *Calgary Herald*, April 5, 1893 and October 23, 1897.

[7] James Short quoted in Robert M. Stamp, *School Days, A Century of Memories* (Calgary: Calgary Board of Education, 1975), p. 18.

[8] When the original house was demolished in 1957, its street address was 1011 4th Avenue SW, at the south end of the Louise Bridge. A smaller replica of the sandstone bungalow was constructed at Heritage Park in 1972.

[9] D. Watson Davis to Daniel Davis, Chester, Vermont, dated Fort Hamilton BA, June 28th 1873, in Lewis O. Saum, ed., "From Vermont to Whoop-Up Country. Some letters of D.W. Davis, 1867-1878," *Montana*, 35, 3 (Summer 1985): 67.

[10] A. Ross Cuthbert to L.W. Herchmer, dated Calgary, August 9, 1892, National Archives of Canada, RG 18, Royal Canadian Mounted Police Records, vol. 69, file 615-1892.

[11] J.H. McIllree to L.W. Herchmer, dated Calgary, January 13, 1890, National Archives of Canada, RG 18, Royal Canadian Mounted Police Records, vol. 39, file 101-1890.

[12] William Beahen, "Andrew Campbell (also known as Dr. Lovingheart)," *Dictionary of Canadian Biography*, vol. 12 (1891-1900) (Toronto: University of Toronto Press, 1990), pp. 154-155.

[15] The motto appears today on the city's official crest. *The Municipal Handbook of Interesting Information and Authoritative Statistics*, published by the City of Calgary in November 1982 contains (p. 14) a full description of Calgary's crest:

"The design for The City of Calgary's official crest was chosen through a contest held by the Calgary Herald, and adopted officially by City Council as the basis for its Corporate Seal in March, 1902. (Bylaw 467).

The upper third of the shield shows the Rocky Mountains an indication of our proximity to those majestic samples of Nature's art. The lower two-thirds bears the red Cross of St. George on which is mounted the Canadian Maple Leaf inset by a bull Buffalo, the former master of our region. The supporters are a horse and a steer, representing the original wealth on which our City was nourished.

The crest above the shield contains a Mural Crown (a symbol of loyalty) and a Westering Sun. Below the shield are the Rose of England, the Thistle of Scotland, and the Shamrock of Ireland, signifying the ancestry of the majority of our early settlers. The scroll contains our motto, "Onward" and the dates of the incorporation of Calgary as a town – 1884, and as a City – 1894. Under the scroll are the Union Jack, signifying our relationship within the British Commonwealth of Nations, and the Canadian Ensign, long used as our country's flag.

The date shown for the incorporation as a town in the original design was 1882. This date was supplied in error at the time the design competition was held. City Council officially changed the date in the design during Calgary's centennial year, 1975."

Calgary's official crest.
Reproduced with the permission of the City of Calgary.

Calgary and its Hinterlands: Ranching, Farming, Oil and Gas

Max Foran

CPR station and Atlantic (9th) Avenue, 1885. Canadian Railway Museum, St. Constant,

In the spring of 1883, the rails of the Canadian Pacific Railroad unfolded westward like twin silver ribbons across the prairies. When they crossed the Elbow River near the fort in August, Calgary's future was assured. "A C.P.R. town and proud of it," became an unofficial town motto in the ensuing thirty years which saw continued rail construction effectively cement Calgary as the largest transportation centre west of Winnipeg. But while the rails tapped both the ranching and agricultural hinterlands, it was not enough. It was left to oil and gas to propel Calgary to "big city" status.

Calgary's focal position as a railroad centre ensured its important role in the settlement process, which began in earnest around the turn of the century. By 1911, the busy warehouse district that sprang up along Ninth and Tenth Avenues adjacent to the tracks contained 150 wholesale and jobbing houses which were filled with the goods and machinery demanded by ranchers, farmers, and the business enterprises that supplied them. Similarly, the construction of stockyards in 1887 and 1903 and subsequent grain-handling facilities reinforced the city's position as a distributing and

15

collecting centre. An enthusiastic Board of Trade realized the crucial importance of railways. In 1908, it called for every man, woman and child in Calgary to take up the cause of railroad promotion.

Calgary's advantages were not lost on the CPR. Switching yards were located just east of the sandstone station and completed in 1905. With over twenty miles of track, and capable of handling 700 cars per day, these yards were worth a million dollars annually to the city. In 1903, the CPR constructed substantial stockyard facilities in east Calgary, and a year later made the city its administrative centre for the extensive irrigation projects in southern Alberta. When the CPR moved its colonization branch and land sales administration to Calgary from Winnipeg in 1910, and two years later established its natural resources department in the city, Calgary's position as a major railway administrative centre was assured.

The opening of the CPR's Palliser Hotel in 1914 as the highest and most impressive building in the city was a symbolic reminder of the premier place the railroad company played in Calgary's urban life, even if it was named after a man who had maintained that no railroad could reach the Pacific without going through the United States.

Yet, arguably perhaps, the CPR's most important contribution to Calgary's overall urban development lay in its long-delayed decision to take advantage of newly generated and cheap hydroelectric power at Horseshoe Falls upriver on the Bow, and locate major locomotive repair and maintenance shops in the city. "We want to be a city," the Calgary Optimist had written before Horseshoe Falls, "and we can't be at $80 per horse power."[1] The giant 213-acre project at Ogden was completed in 1913, and contained twelve buildings designed to repair up to 25 engines and 500 freight cars per month. In addition to providing an incalculable economic boost to the city, the Ogden Shops, by employing 1,200 labourers and skilled tradesmen, helped diversify a largely commercial and service-oriented workforce.

The CPR was a major factor in determining the physical face of the city as well as its later spatial, industrial, commercial and even residential development. Early decisions respecting the opening and closing of railway crossings; the specificity of grants of land for churches and municipal buildings, or for operational facilities like the stockyards and freight yards; or even the placement of both working class and elite residential subdivisions established patterns still observable today. For example, Mount Royal was created as a residential area for the wealthy; Bridgeland for the working class.

By consolidating its presence in the city, the CPR functioned pro-actively as a major employer and participant in urban life, and, more importantly, through its network of lines, it linked Calgary to its hinterlands. The laying of rails to Edmonton in 1891-92, and then to Fort Macleod in 1894, had given Calgary the four-way traffic it needed to achieve regional dominance.

What were the hinterlands served by this railway network? In Calgary's case there were basically two: The pastoral hinterland of the cattle industry and its farming counterpart. The cattle frontier preceded the agricultural and provided Calgary with its first true urban function.

Cutting out cattle on a round-up near High River, 1895. Glenbow Archives/NA-4035-79.

The era of the open range industry really began in 1881 when the first herd of some 3,000 mixed cattle was driven in from Montana to Cochrane, just north of Calgary. Enabled by the federal government's very generous policies allowing large-scale cheap leases, southern Alberta quickly became cattle country.[2] By the end of 1883, more than 25,000 head of cattle ranged between the Bow River and the American border. A year later, there were 1.7 million acres under lease to 41 assorted cattle companies, and by 1906, at the peak of the open range industry, over a million head roamed across three million acres of grasslands fondly described by many of the 1,000 lessees as the finest in the world.

The economic base for a successful open range industry was created by the emergence of a hungry British market for beef. Sales to Britain began in 1888, and over the next twenty years an annual average of 50,000 head of cattle were shipped from Alberta ranches. A more favourable American tariff structure in the 1890s resulted in large-scale cattle movement south of the border. Good prices, cheap leases, and heavy volumes ensured substantial profits and ongoing confidence in the industry's future. For example, the Walrond Ranch north of Pincher Creek realized a clear profit of over $133,000 in 1896. Furthermore, the buoyancy of an industry whose future seemed limitless helped to explain the ranchers' continuing efforts to downplay the agricultural potential of their domains, and, for a time, to delay the opening of the farming frontier.

The cattle industry resulted in Calgary becoming the urban expression of the ranching frontier. Cattle operations demanded centralized facilities for marshalling, marketing, selling and processing. Unlike agriculture, there was a sharp division between the managerial and operational functions, especially on the large spreads. The tightly knit managerial group needed a political, cultural and social milieu typical of large urban centres, and so the Ranchmen's Club with its restricted membership was established in 1892. Its $200 initiation fee guaranteed its members fine food, ten-year-old Edinburgh scotch and the London Times, as well as a proper atmosphere for business dealings.

Calgary's first manufacturing enterprises in the 1890s were based on products associated with the cattle industry. The stockyards, slaughterhouses, and meat packing and processing plants, cold storage facilities, soap-works and tannery, gave east Calgary an industrial appearance, and provided tangible evidence to local boosters that the young city was well on its way to becoming "the Chicago of Canada." In the 1890s, it was chiefly ranching money that built many of the fine sandstone blocks advertising Calgary as "the sandstone city."[3] Put into this context, the comment in 1911 by Pat Burns, rancher and Calgary's first millionaire, that he "had made Calgary" probably contained more truth than modesty.

The Calgary Stockyards, around 1930. Glenbow Archives/NA-554-29.

But though the more realistic ranchers might have realized that their open range kingdoms could not forever withstand the pressure of the settlement frontier, and that the inevitable presence of the latter would necessitate significant land-use changes, it was Mother Nature that really signalled the end of an era. The harsh climate had periodically exacted its toll over the years. The original Cochrane herd was virtually wiped out in 1881-82, while the winter of 1886-87 was not only catastrophic in terms of stock losses, but also effectively deterred American cattlemen from stocking the Canadian range.

However severe other winters may have been, they were nothing compared to the winter of 1906-07. It started early with layers of fall sleet coating rangelands already denuded by persistent summer fires, and when spring temperatures finally melted the snow and ice, and eroded the drifts, thousands of carcasses were left strewn across the bare pasture lands or piled grotesquely in coulees.[4] Many ranchers saw their herds depleted by over one-half, and, in the Calgary area, the figure was set at over sixty percent. No one was spared, big or small. One prominent ranch, the Bar U, west of High River, lost one-half of its 24,000 herd.

The open range industry, some ten million dollars poorer, never recovered. Beleaguered increasingly by a federal government committed to agricultural development, it gave way to more limited fenced operations and to mixed farming enterprises, and co-existed with the frontier that replaced it. But the golden age was over. When in 1912 four former cattle kings popularly known as the "Big Four" put up $100,000 to hold the First Calgary Stampede, they believed they were throwing a party to farewell a by-gone era, a "last hurrah" if you will. That Calgary continues to utilize the Stampede as a positive identification symbol is an irony the Big Four would doubtless have appreciated.

Cattle remained important to Calgary. Because of the industry's transformed nature, however, the city has lost its regional dominance of ranching. Mixed farming and feedlot operations have done for other centres like Red Deer and Edmonton what the open rangelands formerly did for Calgary. There are other factors to consider as well. Dwarfed by its American counterpart, deprived of a large national consumer market, and subject to furious global competition, the Alberta cattle industry has never realized its original lofty ambitions. The fact that most Alberta cattle were not slaughtered in Calgary limited the expansion of local-related industries. Toronto, not Calgary, became the leading cattle market in Canada. Fluctuating tariff and quota policies in the United States created periodic unease over access to Alberta's biggest beef market. So while Calgary's short-lived but vibrant open range industry may have fuelled the young city's aspirations and infused a strong sense of identification, it has not been a major factor in urban growth since World War I.

The opening of Calgary's agricultural hinterland coincided roughly with the birth of the province in 1905 (and, the ranchers would say, with the disastrous winter of 1906-07). Enabled by a generous homestead system and the development of early ripening Marquis wheat, the West finally came into its own. Some 80,000 acres were under field crops in 1898; by 1910, the figure was 3.3 million acres. Yields were equally impressive. Oat production increased five fold, from 3.7 million bushels in 1900 to 17 million in 1910. The great-

An early farm near Calgary. The William Bruce farm was located where the Brentwood Shopping Centre was built in 1963, just northeast of what is now the campus of The University of Calgary. Glenbow Archives/NA 1097-1.

est gains, however, came in wheat production, where yields went from less than 800,000 bushels in 1900 to 9 million bushels in 1910 and culminated in the bumper crop of 360 million bushels in 1915.

Calgary's population in this pre-1914 boom settlement period reflected hinterland growth, unofficially topping the 50,000 mark in 1912. The city became the regional headquarters for agricultural implement dealers, commercial travellers and financial houses. Hotels and boarding houses proliferated. The city's manufacturing base jumped 1,500 percent in the decade 1900-10 by mainly catering to local and regional demands. Lumber, foundry products, flour, processed meats, beer, soap, sandstone and bricks made their way from Calgary producers to the small towns and rural areas of southern Alberta. Even amid the lean economic times of the post-war period, local promoters were successful in luring Spillers Ltd.,

American settlers on Stephen (8th) Avenue, early 1900s. Glenbow Archives/ NA-1126-2.

the British milling giant, to the city in 1924, and the Pioneer Tractor Company in 1929, while in 1933 Calgary possessed the only oatmeal processing plant in Alberta.

Calgary interests aggressively pursued policies favourable to hinterland development. The Board of Trade (now the Chamber of Commerce) protested a federal freight rate structure that jeopardized the development of an integrated western economy in favour of eastern manufacturing interests. The Board lobbied for the alternative Pacific route for western grain. It also held seed competitions and tried to protect the sugar beet industry by lobbying for duties on imported sugar. As the headquarters of organizations formed both by stockgrowers and by farmers to guard their collective interests, Calgary filled a typically metropolitan role as spokesperson for its hinterland.

Sustained growth in this agricultural hinterland, and in Calgary, was dependent, however, on the rural population increase provided by an expanding frontier, as well as by continued crop productivity, and favourable market conditions. But none of this occurred. After 1915, Calgary's long-held vision of big city status vanished as rural Alberta went into serious economic decline.

The outbreak of World War I ended the immigration boom and closed the settlement frontier. Then, following the war, drought, inflation and collapsing agricultural prices sent Alberta and western Canada "rushing heedlessly, unknowingly into the very jaws of the most crushing debacle recorded in the history of the west."[5] In south-eastern Alberta, 140 townships had lost 55 percent of their population by 1926. In 1923, a CPR official admitted that 80 percent of Alberta's farmers were bankrupt. To City Clerk Jim Miller, 1923 was Calgary's worst year ever. In 1916-17, southern Alberta's grain crop was over 37 million bushels. It was under 4 million bushels in 1919, and

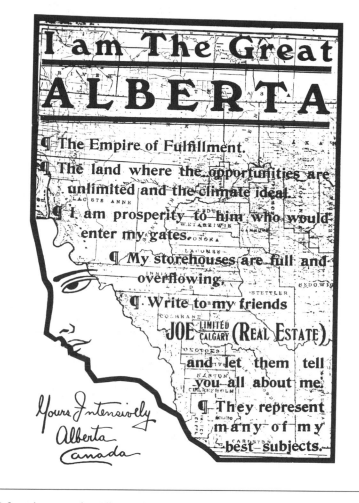

Advertisement for Alberta in the Calgary Herald, June 1910. Glenbow Archives/NA-789-21.

well under 10 million bushels in the early 1920s. Prices fell just as dramatically. From over $2 per bushel in 1917-18, the price of No. 1 Northern wheat plummeted to well under $1 in the early 1920s and 1930s, and generally remained depressed until the Second World War.

Calgary mirrored the woes of its hinterland during this period, suffering severe unemployment problems, rising retail prices, and a dwindling tax base. With the collapse of the real estate and construction boom, it was freely admitted that the wholesale trade was all the city had to fall back on. By 1926, it was generally conceded that the "good old days" were gone forever. Between 1916 and 1940, the only two reasonably good years for grain and cattle occurred in 1928 and 1929, and Calgary quickly reflected this short-lived upswing with increased retail sales and new commercial and industrial construction. City Commissioner Arthur Graves' effusive remark "that 1929 was the best year ever" for Calgary was simply an unwitting recognition of the close ties between urban and hinterland economic health.

In modern times, rural depopulation has not diminished the importance of agriculture in Alberta. Yet, with the exception of irrigation areas, southern Alberta was, and still is, risky cash crop country. The rural hinterland that helped build and sustain Calgary had not the potential dreamed of and touted by the local promoters. Like other global areas reliant on export products, Calgary's hinterland depended upon the uncontrollable variables associated with climate and international supply and demand. In the pre-1914 boom period, Calgary had a 100,000, and later a Quarter Million, Club. It should be remembered that the slow, even modest, growth of a city that increased in population from 4,000 in 1900 to over 50,000 by 1912—but which did not reach the magic 100,000 until 1946—was linked as much with limited hinterland potential as it was with the closing of the settlement frontier. Edmonton's richer agricultural hinterland gives it more stability than Calgary's.

It was left to oil and gas to do for Calgary what cattle and agriculture could not. The fact that Saskatchewan's population exceeded Alberta's by 100,000 as late as 1941 represents a clear statement

The Turner Valley oil wells, 1920s. Glenbow Archives/NC-26-325.

that Calgary's and Edmonton's current population has little to do with its agricultural or ranching hinterlands. The city had, however, benefited from Alberta's initial modest oil strike at Turner Valley south-west of the city in 1914. Through Turner Valley,

Calgary's skyline after the oil boom burst in the early 1980s. Calgary Sun, February 20, 1983.

Canadian oil expertise was built up and controlled in Calgary. The city functioned as headquarters for the numerous companies probing Turner Valley and other areas of southern Alberta. By 1940, Calgary counted two refineries, and, far more importantly, the recently established Petroleum and Natural Gas Conservation Board. Thus when Imperial Oil finally tapped the sizeable reservoirs in the Devonian reef in February 1947 and ushered in the modern oil era, Calgary was ready to reap the rewards.

Calgary's growth paralleled that of Alberta's new industry. Annual oil production in the province rose from 6.3 million barrels in 1946 to over 522 million barrels in 1973. In the same period, Calgary's population increased fourfold to well over 400,000, by 1981 it approached 600,000, and went above 700,000 by 1991. As the managerial headquarters of a burgeoning industry, the city became the third-ranking centre in Canada in terms of head offices and as a main focus for inter-provincial migration. The crucial but disproportionate importance of the oil and natural gas industry in Calgary is reflected in a multiplier effect that at one point may have designated seven jobs for every one created in the oil patch.

The oil and natural gas industry has enabled Calgary to extend its sphere of influence well beyond provincial boundaries. Companies based in Calgary are active world-wide, whether it be pioneering exploratory activity in Canada's north, preparing the Siberian taiga or Indonesian jungles for drilling, offshore operations in the North Sea, or furnishing portable housing for extensive pipeline, road, or other construction projects. The current emphasis on optimizing American export markets for Alberta natural gas is a further reminder of Calgary's (and Alberta's) continuing reliance on fossil fuel extraction. However, the collapse of oil prices in the mid-1980s and Alberta's minor role as a global policymaker has sobered the booster mentality spawned by the seemingly limitless prosperity of the 1950-80 period.

Cities generally reflect the productivity of their hinterlands, and are differentiated by the degree to which they can widen their metropolitan control to include other cities and/or hinterlands. Over the course of one hundred and ten years, Calgary's crucial position as a transportation centre allowed it to dominate, first a ranching, and then an agricultural hinterland. The limitation of these hinterlands was reflected in modest, even erratic overall growth until the post-Second World War period when they were more than offset by the city's association with the petroleum and natural gas industry. It has been this larger, more prosperous but no less volatile hinterland that has thrust Calgary into the top tier of Canada's urban hierarchy.

Notes

[1] *Calgary Optimist*, December 11, 1909.

[2] For an excellent assessment of the impact of ranching in southern Alberta, see David H. Breen, *The Canadian Prairie West and the Ranching Frontier 1874-1924* (Toronto: University of Toronto Press, 1983).

[3] For information on these sandstone structures, see Richard Cunniffe, *Calgary, The Sandstone City* (Calgary: The Alberta Historical Society, 1969).

[4] L.V. Kelly, *The Range Men* (Toronto: Thomas Briggs, 1913), pp. 376-380.

[5] David Jones, ed. *"We'll all be buried down here," The Prairie Dryland Disaster 1917-1926* (Calgary: Alberta Records Publication Board and The Historical Society of Alberta, 1986), p. 22.

Native Peoples and Calgary

Hugh Dempsey

The Indians were an integral part of the Calgary area long before there was a police fort or a town. The region abounds in archaeological remains, including butchering sites, buffalo jumps, and tipi rings, which indicate that Indians found the area between the Bow and Elbow rivers to be an excellent campsite and a safe river crossing. In summer, the surrounding hills and western breezes provided relief from heat and the myriad of mosquitoes and other pests, while in winter the valley was often bathed in warm chinook winds.

An Indian camp on the Elbow River, late 1880s. Boorne and May photo. Glenbow Archives/NA-1753-50.

Evidence of the antiquity of occupation in the area was provided in 1968, when stone tools were discovered while excavating for the Mona Lisa Art Gallery at 17th Avenue near 7th Street SW. They were nine feet below the surface and tests indicated that hunters had been butchering at this site more than 8,000 years ago. Artifacts also have been found in Hawkwood, Parkdale, Point Mackay, Bow Bottom, Strathcona Park, and at other locations. At Fish Creek Park alone, some 46 prehistoric sites have been recorded, with another 42 on Nose Hill.[1]

When the whisky traders and missionaries arrived in the early 1870s, they found that the Blackfoot[2] and Bloods were the tribes that most often wintered in the area. The first Catholic missionaries who came in 1873 found a band of Bloods under Rainy Chief settled along the Elbow for the winter. During that same period, Red Crow, head chief of the Bloods, traded with the Americans, who had a post farther downstream on that river.

When the North-West Mounted Police built Fort Calgary in 1875, three companies—Hudson's Bay, I.G. Baker, and T.C. Power—built trading stores to serve their buffalo hunting customers. These were mostly from the Blackfoot and Sarcee[3] tribes; the Stoneys frequented the store at Morley, while the Bloods and Peigans took their trade to Fort Macleod. The establishment of the Mounted Police fort also brought a number of Cree Metis hunters to the area. They built cabins near the Catholic mission on the Elbow River and established Calgary's first permanent village. Some of these Metis included the families of Louis Roselle, "Little Paul" Faillant, John Ward, Henry Pauquet, Augustus Gouin, and John Monroe. They hunted, trapped, and did odd jobs for the police and traders.

The existence of the Police at the forks had a profound impact on the Sarcees. When they signed Treaty Seven in 1877, they were persuaded to share a large reserve with the Blackfoot, but when the buffalo were killed off, they realized that they did not want to be that cosy with their one-time allies. They were permitted to spend the winter of 1879-80 near the fort, provided they worked at the Fish Creek farm, which had been established just south of Calgary by the Indian Department. The Sarcees liked the area so much that their chief, Bull Head, waged a two-year struggle to have their reserve moved to Fish Creek. Finally, the government acquiesced and the Sarcees were given three townships of land along the creek south-west of the town. They became Calgary's closest Indian neighbours.

During the 1870s and early 1880s, the Indians were important to Calgary's economic well-being, their trade in buffalo robes keeping the trading stores busy. For example, in 1878, Hudson's Bay trader Angus Fraser commented, "I have taken in $130 cash 125 Prime Buffalo Robes besides other fur and leather."[4] But with the disappearance of the buffalo herds, the situation drastically changed. The importance of the Indians to Calgary was then limited to the issuing of government contracts for beef and flour, thus providing local employment for ranchers, freighters, and other workers.

The once-independent Indians became impoverished and indigent, forced onto their reserves if they wished to receive government rations. They soon became victims of government bureaucracy, requiring permission to leave their reserves and to sell their products. The only way an Indian could legally go outside of his reserve was with a pass from the Indian agent. This document indicated where he was going, how many in his party, and the purpose of his trip. One such permit, for example, indicated that "Bull Horn & party of Five of Blood Band is permitted to be absent from his Reserve for Ten days from date hereof. Business to hunt and get logs and [he] is permitted to carry a gun."[5] Similar permits were required if an Indian was going to sell any hay, grain or cattle from the reserve. These permits were used well into the twentieth century. One example in 1913 stated, "Dick Starlight is hereby permitted to sell 1 Load Hay"; it was signed by the Indian agent.[6]

Any Indians encountered off their reserve could be challenged by a Mounted Policeman, and if they failed to have the correct permits they could be arrested and either jailed or sent back home. In 1884, Superintendent Sam Steele wrote from Calgary, "I have made arrangements with the Indian agent that no Indians are to be allowed to stay here without a permit from him; these permits to be granted sparingly, and only when absolutely necessary."[7] Yet

Camp of Sarcee Indians, with Calgary in the background. Glenbow Archives/NA-468-15.

the rules were not always rigidly enforced. In 1887, there were 34 lodges of Crees, Blackfoot, and Sarcees camped around the town. "They claim they are working," commented the police.[8]

There were three main Native camp grounds in the Calgary area. The largest was along the Elbow River near the Catholic mission. This was a favourite area of the Crees and Metis, many of whom were nominally Catholics. A few of the long-time residents lived in comfortable log cabins, while others preferred skin tipis. The area from Elbow, extending along the base of what is now Mount Royal, was a camping area for Sarcee Indians, who periodically came from their reserve to trade, spend their treaty money, or sell such items as berries, Christmas trees, and fence posts.

The second Indian community was at Shaganappi Point, in the area east of the present Shaganappi golf course. The term "Shaganappi" referred to untanned leather that was often used by the Metis for ropes or repairing Red River carts. This area was occupied primarily by Crees and Metis, although Stoneys coming from their reserve at Morley also camped there. The

27

third campsite was on the north side of the Bow River near the mouth of Nose Creek. While a few Cree and Sarcee may have stayed there, this was primarily a Blackfoot encampment. Indians coming from the Blackfoot Reserve pitched their lodges, then crossed Langevin bridge to do their shopping. A painting by John Hammond completed in the early 1890s shows a camp of tipis just south of the present General Hospital. During the 1890s, the nominal leader of the Nose Creek village was Deerfoot, a champion Blackfoot runner who often competed in Calgary races.

For a few years after 1885, the number of Cree Indians in the area swelled when Bobtail, a chief from Hobbema, withdrew most of his band from treaty status after a dispute with the government. This meant that they were no longer under the restrictions of the Indian Act and the authorities could not send them away because they had no reserve to go to. Members of this band, consisting at its peak of some twenty lodges, eked out a living by working in local abattoirs and lumber mills, while others turned to begging and prostitution.

John Hammond, "View near Calgary," completed around 1894. Glenbow Museum/987.97.1 (photo no. 14644).

An infamous incident occurred in 1889 when a young prostitute from the Cree camp, Rosalie New Grass, was murdered by a local gambler. Such was the discrimination directed towards Indians that the first jury declared the gambler to be not guilty in spite of overwhelming evidence. The Calgary Tribune said the verdict was a disgrace to Calgary. "The idea which seems to possess the minds of some people," said the editor, "that because a crime or offence is committed against an Indian, therefore the crime is lessened, is inhuman in the extreme."[9] Judge Rouleau agreed; he refused to accept the verdict and sentenced the killer to fourteen years in prison after a second jury found him guilty.

For the next several years, the image which many Calgarians had of Indians was a negative one, based on the indigent people

Pupils of the Calgary Industrial School, 1907. The principal, the Rev. George Hogbin, is the man standing at the extreme right in the last row. Glenbow Archives/NA-75-2.

seen on the streets and the shadow that hung over them because of the 1885 rebellion. In 1900, a Calgary Herald reporter noted that most Calgarians saw Indians as people who were "scavenging around the towns and villages, arrayed in squalid garments, engaged in disgusting occupations, and sunk in stolid misery."[10]

Yet in the 1890s, a more positive image began to appear with the construction of the Calgary Indian Industrial School. Located on the Bow River, the school was run by the Anglican Church and brought the brightest and the best Native students to Calgary's doorstep. The school consisted of a four-storey sandstone building, carpenter and printing shop, bakery, principal's house, farm instructor's house, barn, and outbuildings, all on three hundred acres of land which fronted on the river.

Much of this land is now under Deerfoot Trail in southeast Calgary.

The school was officially opened by the Governor General, Lord Aberdeen, on December 9, 1896. No students had yet been enrolled, so the first principal, the Rev. George Hogbin, "borrowed" a number of pupils from the nearby Sarcee Reserve.

Calgary Industrial could accommodate fifty boys between the ages of twelve and eighteen. The idea was to take them away from the influences of their reserves and teach them such trades as farming, carpentry, blacksmithing, and printing, as well as academic subjects. In addition, they became a visible part of the Calgary community as they put on demonstrations, competed in sporting events, and were hailed as examples of successful government policies.

The first love of the students was football, and within a year or two, they began winning games on a regular basis. The league included the Calgary fire brigade, brewery, city police, railway workers, and two professional teams, the Albions and the Caledonians. The most challenging competitors were the Caledonians, who could be as rough on the playing field as the industrial school team. In 1898, the industrial school boys won a silver tankard, a challenge cup, and a set of championship medals in their games against Calgary teams.

The students were encouraged to mix with townspeople. They sometimes went to church at Midnapore or Calgary, put on concerts, and were allowed to work for local farmers and ranchers. Some of the outstanding boys were also invited to take part in ceremonies in town. In 1901, for example, Sarcee student David

Wolf Carrier presented the address of welcome to the Duke and Duchess of Cornwall and York during their vice-regal visit to Calgary.

Another positive image of Indians in Calgary began at the turn of the century at summer fairs and holiday events such as Queen Victoria's Birthday and Dominion Day. On these occasions, Sarcee Indians were invited to join the parades in full costume and to offer demonstrations of dancing, archery, racing, or other activities. Many of these programs were organized by James "Cappy" Smart, the city's fire chief, who established good relations with the tribes in the surrounding area.

The exhibitions were organized, of course, for the entertainment of the townspeople, but the Indians thoroughly enjoyed the chance to participate. It gave them an opportunity to relieve the monotony of reservation life and enabled them to be paid either in food or cash for their services. These activities became the forerunners of the Calgary Stampede.

However, Native participation in Calgary festivities did not come easily. By 1910, the government had concluded that such participation was counter-productive to their program of turning the Indians into farmers and ranchers. The fairs often occurred when the government wanted the Indians to be busy haying or working in their fields. Officials also saw the events as an encouragement for Indians to retain old customs which, in their opinion, had no place in the new world that the government had laid out for them.

In 1912, the government tried to prevent Indians from taking part in the first Calgary Stampede. However, the political influence of James Lougheed and R.B. Bennett, both Calgarians, convinced the Superintendent-General of Indian Affairs to allow the Indians to attend the gala event. In spite of complaints from Indian agents and some religious groups, the Rev. John McDougall helped organize the largest Indian show ever seen in the city. The Toronto *Globe* commented approvingly that the "gorgeous display of paint, beads and colored blankets was made by the six tribes of Indians who formed the bulk of the parade, and lent a historic picturesqueness to the modern city street with its thousands of thronging spectators."[11]

During the six-day event, the Indians were everywhere. Their tipis were located next to replicas of a Hudson's Bay Company post and they offered daily dances and joined in parades. At the grandstand performances, they put on a spectacular show, while in the rodeo events, Tom Three Persons became the only Canadian champion when he won the bronco riding competition.

Indians in the Stampede Parade, 1912. View from the east of 1st Street W., looking west. Glenbow Archives/NA-4035-96.

Officials estimated that 1,800 Indians had attended the six-day Stampede; yet there had only been seven arrests under the Indian Act—all for liquor offences—during the entire period. This caused an Indian Department official to comment that "if the white men who were in Calgary during that week had been under the same [liquor] regulation ... there would not have been jails enough in Canada to hold them."[12]

The Calgary Exhibition and Stampede did not become an annual event until 1923, but by that time the government had given up on enforcing its restrictions against fairs and rodeos. Each year the tipi village was pitched under the huge Sun Tree at the entrance to the grounds and became one of the highlights of the fair. With the expansion of the Stampede in 1974, it was moved to a more secluded place at the south end, where tribal members were

The University of Calgary's first convocation, May 26, 1966. In the front row is Dr. Ruth Gorman (on the left) and President Herb Armstrong (on the right), the first president of The University of Calgary. In the centre sits Tatanga Mani (Walking Buffalo), a Stoney Indian, born in March 1871. Tatanga Mani had seen the last buffalo herds in this area. As Grant MacEwan writes in his biography of him (Tatanga Mani, p. 48): "Buffalo herds disappeared before Walking Buffalo was old enough to pursue them in the role of hunter, but he accompanied the older hunters as a child and could recall the slaughter, the hours spent in skinning, and the odour of meat drying in the sun." Daisy and David Crowchild appear in the back row on the left, with Howard and Mabel Beebe, Blood Indians, on the right. Walking Buffalo, the Crowchilds and the Beebes had come to the ceremony at which their friend, Ruth Gorman, had been awarded an honorary doctorate. University Archives, The University of Calgary.

able to pitch their lodges in a park-like atmosphere beside the Elbow River.

Over the years, the Calgary Stampede has been the main showcase for the pageantry and grandeur of the southern Alberta Indians. It has become a source of pride, both for the Stampede and for the Indian people. Many Native families are quick to point out today that they are the second or third generation of participants, that their parents or grandparents took part in the first Stampede. They exhibit their skills in beadwork, painted tipis, and crafts, and vie for the trophies, which are awarded annually.

The Stampede years have not been without controversy but the problems were usually resolved without too much rancour. In 1950, there was trouble when the Stampede ended its practice of giving all Indians free admission to the grounds. When the Stoneys boycotted the event, a rumour was spread that they had held a "rain dance," which resulted in a heavy downpour during Stampede week. It was all nonsense, of course. As patriarch Tom Kaquitts noted, "The rains were not caused by the Indians but came from someone above, far over the blue mountains."[13] Over the winter, the matter was resolved and the tribe was back the following year.

Another problem arose in 1965 when the poor location of the village caused it to be flooded during a heavy rainstorm. This was before it was moved to its present location. Many valuable costumes and personal possessions were damaged or destroyed and when compensation was not immediately forthcoming, some of the owners formed a union-like United Indian Committee to handle their grievances. However, the Stampede would deal only with individual owners and ultimately settled with them.

A more serious confrontation took place in 1972, when Dave and Daisy Crowchild, two of the most popular people in the village, were suspended for a year and their tipi site was given to someone else. The problem arose when the couple was invited to a Native ceremony and moved out of the village before the Stampede was over. Even though they left their tipi in place, they were told they had broken the rules and were being punished.

There was a great outcry from the general public, for the Crowchilds were among the leading goodwill ambassadors between the Native and white communities. Finally, an invitation was extended for them to return, but they never did.

Then there was a further controversy in 1991 when Bruce Starlight, chairman of the Indian Events Committee, was passed over in an election for a seat on the prestigious Stampede Board of Directors. Stung by criticism in the press and from the public, the Stampede in 1992 named Roy Whitney, chief of the Sarcee tribe, to fill one of the appointed seats on the Board of Directors, and later in the year Starlight was finally elected to fill one of the other vacancies.

Yet when an outsider complains about the village, the Indians close ranks. On one occasion, a Calgary alderman said the Indians were being exploited and were being used as "tourist gimmicks."[14] Wilfred Mark, of the Stoney tribe, was among the first to jump to the defence of the Stampede. "Nobody forces us to take part," he said. "We do it because we enjoy it and look forward to going every year. While we camp there, we have a chance to see a lot of things and do some visiting. It is especially nice for Indian youngsters."[15] George Runner, from the Sarcee tribe, agreed. "I hope my children will take over after me," he said, "and keep up our family participation in the Stampede."

This participation has not been limited to parades and tipis. From the beginning, Indians have played a major role in the rodeo events, and contestants such as Pete Bruised Head, Jim Wells, Fred and Jim Gladstone, Edgar Baptiste, and Rae Mitsuing have become prominent names in rodeo history. Other Indians have participated in the school fairs and art shows sponsored by the Stampede.

The 1960s saw a major change in Indian-Calgary relations when the general rural-to-urban trend extended to the Native communities. Seeking better opportunities than those existing on reserves, Indians began to move into the city from southern Alberta reserves and from other parts of the prairie provinces. Among the first were teenaged students who were brought to the city by the Department of Indian Affairs to obtain the kind of high school and college education which was not available on reserves. This was followed by a general influx of Natives, and in 1964 the Calgary Indian Friendship Centre was established to meet their needs. In succeeding years, other Native organizations made their appearance, such as Native Outreach, Calgary Urban Treaty Indian Alliance, Native Counselling Services of Alberta, Native Employment Transitional Services, and various alcohol and drug rehabilitation programs.

The 1960s and 1970s were years of unrest, with the American Indian Movement leading a sit-in of the Department of Indian Affairs in 1974 and a mass rally a short time later. A number of Indians began attending The University of Calgary and Mount Royal College, while others were employed by local oil companies and professional businesses.

Meanwhile, the Sarcee Reserve continued to be a good neighbour. By the 1990s, the city had extended to the reserve's eastern boundary and was beginning to surround it. The tribe changed its name to the Tsuu T'ina Nation and launched an impressive economic development program. It began in 1972 with Redwood Mead-

Linda Fraser, Lawrence Whitney, and Ted Lee display the sign that is to identify the new Indian Friendship Centre at 140, 2nd Street SW. Calgary Herald photo, August 4, 1966. Glenbow Archives/NA-2864-1295-2.

ows, a residential sub-division and adjoining golf course at the west end of the reserve. In 1984, the band formed Sarcee Gravel Products, serving a large number of customers in Calgary and surrounding rural areas. It also built the Seven Chiefs Sports-Plex and the Harry Dodging Horse Memorial Agri-Plex, as well as forming the Tsuu T'ina Cattle Company, and Tsuu T'ina Mechanical, together earning about $15 million annually.

In 1992, the Tsuu T'ina Nation took another step forward with a $15 million construction project at the point where Anderson Road enters the reserve. When the project is completed, it will include a 27-hole golf course, a large multi-purpose retail and office complex, restaurant, bank, supermarket, motor vehicles office, and an expanded service station. Space in the office building has already been leased to the Treaty Seven Tribal Office, Indian Oil and Gas Canada, Indian Health and Welfare Canada, and a number of Indian-owned businesses.

Meanwhile, the city of Calgary is home to an increasing number of Natives. Today, there are more than 20,000 from all parts of Canada. Some are employed in the oil industry and professional firms, while others may be found in all levels of business and society. There are about 250 students attending The University of Calgary, and others at Mount Royal College, SAIT, and Alberta Vocational College.

In recognition of the ongoing relationship between the Native and non-Native peoples, the City of Calgary established the Chief David Crowchild Memorial Award in 1986. It honours selected citizens for creating a better understanding in the fields of Native culture, education, training, employment and self-fulfillment, and for "encouraging cross-cultural experiences between native and non-native communities."[16] The first recipient was Pauline Dempsey, a member of the Blood tribe who has an outstanding record for Native community service in the city. Since that time, a permanent record of the annual award winners has been placed on a sculpture at the main entrance to the Municipal Building. This would seem to be a fitting place to recognize old friends and neighbours.

Notes

[1] Michael C. Wilson and Kenneth J. Hardy, "The Archaeology of the Calgary Area, Alberta," in *Geology of the Calgary Area* (eds. L.E. Jackson Jr. and M.C. Wilson). Calgary: Canadian Society of Petroleum Geologists, 1987, p. 131.

[2] This tribe currently uses the term "Siksika Nation."

[3] This tribe currently uses the term "Tsuu T'ina Nation."

[4] Angus Fraser to Richard Hardisty, November 20, 1878. Hardisty papers, No. 1058, Glenbow Archives.

[5] Blood Indian Agency Papers, Glenbow Archives.

[6] Permit, July 2, 1913, in author's possession.

[7] S.B. Steele to Commissioner, May 24, 1884. RCMP Papers, RG 18, vol. 1016, f.1262, National Archives of Canada (NAC).

[8] W.M. Herchmer to Commissioner, June 4, 1887. RCMP Papers, RG 18, vol. 1077, F. 321, NAC.

[9] *Calgary Tribune*, June 17, 1889.

[10] *Calgary Weekly Herald*, October 4, 1900.

[11] *The Globe*, Toronto, September 4, 1912.

[12] Glen Campbell to Hon. Thomas Crothers, May 12, 1913. Indian Affairs, RG 10, vol. 3826, file 60, 511-3, NAC.

[13] *Calgary Herald*, December 8, 1950.

[14] Idem., February 18, 1972.

[15] Idem., February 21, 1972.

[16] Mayor Ralph Klein to Pauline Dempsey, October 27, 1986. In recipient's possession.

Cultural Life in Calgary in the Twentieth Century

Kathleen M. Snow

Of all the arts, music has had the first and most lasting attraction for the citizens of Calgary. Many immigrants played musical instruments and brought them to Calgary and those who could sing gravitated to the choirs in the various churches. Trained organists and choir masters were hired and organs by Casavant were ordered from Quebec. A spirit of friendly rivalry existed between the choirs as they performed concerts, often of ambitious works such as Elgar's *Dream of Gerontius* or *Hiawatha* by Coleridge-Taylor.

Two notable conductors, both from Britain, dominated the scene in the early twentieth century: P.L. Newcombe of the Apollo Choir and Clifford Higgin, organist of Knox Presbyterian Church. Higgin enthusiastically supported the Alberta Festival Association which held its competitions in varying locations in the province, where these well-attended functions generated high excitement. Higgin also helped to found the Calgary

Amelita Galli-Curci's recital under the sponsorship of the Calgary Women's Musical Association, October 16, 1926. Glenbow Archives/NA-4019-9.

Music Competition Festival, which evolved into the modern Calgary Kiwanis Musical Festival.

The Calgary Women's Musical Association, formed in 1904, provided an opportunity for local and national musicians to perform, and it developed an audience for chamber music and solo concerts. The group convened their meetings in various halls until the luxurious Palliser Hotel was built, and they could meet in a large room at the Palliser on the mezzanine floor. There the ladies sat on gilt chairs with their elaborate hats and listened to French Art songs, *lieder*, and instrumental concerts. Mrs. H.H. Sharples, one of the most influential leaders of this organization, initiated an annual performance of local composers' work. She also began a concert series under the Association's sponsorship. Calgarians heard violinist Fritz Kreisler, the coloratura soprano Amelita Galli-Curci and Calgary-born Kathleen Parlow, an internationally known virtuoso.

As the Royal Schools of Music's local representative Mrs. Sharples made the arrangements for an examiner from Britain to conduct the candidates' examinations for the degree and the awarding of scholarships. An impressive number of young Calgary musicians were able to take advantage of expert training in England. The majority returned to Calgary to perform, teach, and play in the Calgary Symphony Orchestra. The Mount Royal Conservatory of Music and Speech Arts was formed in 1910 and attracted talented instructors to the great benefit of their many local pupils.

A small symphony orchestra was formed in 1910 with the Calgary's famous violinist Kathleen Parlow as a member. It was enlarged after the First World War to a viable orchestra with 75 members under conductor Gregori Garbovitsky, whose entertain-

ing eccentricities complemented his considerable musical abilities. During one long and strenuous rehearsal of Lalo's *Symphonie Espagnol,* he stood with his hair dye mingling with the perspiration on his forehead. Suddenly aware of the exhaustion of the members of the orchestra he stopped abruptly, and ordered ice cream for everyone.

The symphony orchestra, Calgary, in the early 1900s. Kathleen Parlow is the young woman seated first on the left in the front row. Glenbow Archives/NA-2996-5.

Local singers also became involved in musical theatre, the productions often directed and sometimes acted in by Mrs. Roland Winter, an impressive Edwardian figure usually draped in violet veils. They had fun staging such works as Gilbert and Sullivan's *The Pirates of Pensance* at Hull's Opera House, then the finest theatre on the prairies. Subsequently, performances of all kinds were held in Sherman's Opera House and the Sherman Grand Theatre, which at the time had the largest stage in Canada. When Sir James Lougheed bought the Grand Theatre, he opened it with Forbes Robertson playing in *The Third Floor Back*. Robertson's was one of the many travelling companies such as the D'Oyly Carte and the San Carlo Opera, which could be accommodated in the elaborately

Cast of the "Mikado" on stage, Lyric Theatre, Calgary, February 23, 1911. Glenbow Archives/NA-3927-2.

Hull's Opera House, built by William Roper Hull in 1893. Glenbow Archives/NA-468-4.

decorated theatre with the scene from Shakespeare's *As You Like It* painted on the fire curtain. Sir John Martin Harvey thrilled audiences with *A Tale of Two Cities* or *The Bells*. Packed houses greeted such celebrities as the Australian soprano Nellie Melba, the English contralto Clara Butt, and the great Russian dancer, Pavlova, considered the finest ballerina of her time. Later, the Sir Barry Jackson troupe with their accomplished players and productions gave Calgarians such classics as *Dear Brutus*, *She Stoops to Conquer*, and *Quality Street*. The Abbey Players from Dublin performed *Playboy of the Western World* and *Juno and the Paycock*.

These companies set a high standard of theatrical entertainment, but it was the Chautauqua which involved local talent. Calgary became one of the Chautauqua's organizing centres. Here the directors chose attractive, capable women to visit small communities and persuade the local authorities to back a week of entertainment. A huge tent was set up in a vacant field and tickets sold for the performances of concert par-

The Calgary Public or Carnegie Library, around 1912/ Glenbow Archives/NA-4385-6.

ties, lectures, plays and novelty acts. For many on the prairies, Chautauqua provided the only introduction they had to the wider cultural world. In Calgary, the Chautauqua tent rose on the grounds of Haultain School. In spite of the heat and the dust, such plays as *The Late Mr. Bean* or *What Every Woman Knows* and the musical performances by accomplished soloists or concert parties enthralled audiences.

Across from Haultain school stood the Calgary Public or Carnegie Library, set in a formal park with a bandstand at one end. Conceived as a classical structure in the familiar local sandstone, the library had pillars, large windows, and an acanthus leaf trim crowning all. Inside, marble and mahogany appeared in the reading rooms, which had fireplaces. This cultural acquisition came to the city as a result of the work of the Calgary Women's Literary Club, formed in 1906. Their leader, Mrs. Annie Davidson wanted Calgary to have a public library, and the Club members canvassed the population of the city for signatures to petitions. Some people, especially working people, were often reluctant to sign because of the American industrialist Andrew Carnegie's hostility to organized labour. However, enough citizens signed and the Carnegie Foundation gave a grant to build the library, which opened in 1912. Since then, the Club has used it as their meeting place. The building, one of the last of the Carnegie libraries on the continent, survived because of the benign neglect of the city fathers, who for years were reluctant to construct a new library. Today, it is fully renovated and preserved as a heritage building.

Although the ladies of the Literary Club initially concentrated on Shakespeare and Browning, several of their members published short stories and poetry and led discussions on Canadian writers, such as Nellie McClung, the most prominent author in the city. The inimitable Bob Edwards' social satire was read by everyone when he published his newspaper, the Eye Opener.

Alexander Calhoun chose the best of contemporary literature for the library's shelves. A selfless social activist himself with great determination and organizing ability, Calhoun knew the needs of the various cultural and intellectual movements in the city. He built a quality collection of books and a staff which supported them. The city's first librarian also organized the first art exhibition, choosing the paintings from private collections in the city and gathering them up with a horse and dray cart. When the Calgary Art Club sought a meeting place, they found one in the library, as well as space for a life-drawing class. Two members of that class, Maxwell Bates and Leroy Stevenson, read every art book in the library and developed as pioneer expressionists and modernists. Their work became celebrated throughout Canada. Their class at the Carnegie Library had ended when a local alderman objected to a nude model.

Bates and Stevenson attended the first classes of Lars Haukaness, the founder of the Alberta College of Art, housed in the Provincial Institute of Technology and Art. A.C. Leighton succeeded him. His summer schools at Banff were a prelude to the summer art school at the Banff School of Fine Arts, established in 1933 under the wing of the University of Alberta to encourage the development of theatre arts. A brilliant, inspiring woman, Elizabeth Sterling Haynes was appointed to head the school, which thrived under her leadership. The curriculum included acting, stagecraft, voice training, directing and creative writing. Local theatre groups in prairie locations, including Calgary, benefited by the entry of trained people. In Calgary, the Green Room Club and the Calgary Civic Theatre struggled through the years of the Depression and World War II with enthusiasm but inadequate facilities.

At Western Canada High School, Betty Mitchell trained her drama students to speak, act, direct, and create scenery. Her student production of *Our Town* was a triumph. She followed it by numerous productions, giving the students wide experience. Betty Mitchell inspired a number of her protégés to pursue careers in the professional theatre, and to that end she formed them into a drama group, Workshop 14. A number of their productions won prizes in the Alberta Drama Festival and the Dominion Drama Festival. Approximately sixty of her students pursued careers in professional theatre.

Calgary's pre-war cultural ferment laid the base for post-war developments. The war years proved a period of shortages, of cutting back and making do, but most of the cultural initiatives survived and were ready to grow.

After the war ended, Alexander Calhoun brought together a small group of Calgarians interested in cultural affairs. They chaired a Civic Centre Committee, which persuaded the city to rent the Coste

The Coste House, 1940s. The director Archie F. Keys is standing on the steps. Glenbow Archives/NA-1427-2.

House, a beautiful, roomy mansion on extensive grounds, which had been occupied by the art school during the war. The Committee became the Allied Arts Council, and under A.F. Key, the dynamic director, lovingly cleaned and restored Coste House with volunteer help. After it opened in 1946, it became a meeting centre for all the cultural groups in the city, and a location for children's art classes. It contained an etching press in the basement, a room for weaving on an upper floor, an art gallery, a location for chamber music in the foyer, and an area for ballet classes. Tea was offered in the conservatory. The Coste House experiment became a model for similar developments all over the continent. It proved such a success that the Canada Council funded an informative brochure for distribution to interested communities.

In one of the Coste House's charming rooms the artist John Snow, Maxwell Bates, Alexander Calhoun and others initiated the Calgary Film Society to show foreign films, providing a contrast to the saccharine products of Hollywood. This very successful organization lasted for over forty years. Maxwell Bates had returned from his artistically successful years in London and the trials of a World War II prison camp to pursue his art and his profession of architecture. He exerted a quiet but powerful influence on the art community, especially on the younger members then graduating from the Alberta College of Art. Under the direction of the notable artist Illingworth Kerr, ACA became one of the leading art schools in Canada.

Anxious to have a university in their city, Calgarians had tried in 1912 to establish one in the Carnegie Library. It failed, as Edmonton refused to fund a second provincial university and because the great Calgary real estate boom of 1902 to 1912 had burst. This initiative died but was revived when, during the war, Mount Royal College offered the first year of university credit which could be transferred to the University of Alberta. The establishment of the University of Alberta in Calgary after the war greatly strengthened the cultural community in Calgary.

With the discovery in 1947 of the Leduc oil field, Eric L. Harvie, a local entrepreneur, suddenly became wealthy. Interested in history and culture, he generously used his wealth to establish the Glenbow Foundation, an offshoot of which is the Glenbow-Alberta Institute. Its library and archives are a boon to researchers. The Museum houses a fine collection of Canadian art which is displayed from time to time together with travelling exhibitions. He also gave it the largest ever gift presented to a cultural institution in Canada: a collection of artifacts from all over the world.

A further gift from Harvie resulted in Heritage Park on the banks of the Elbow River. Here have been assembled pioneer

Maxwell Bates, 1953. Photo from Maxwell Bates fonds. Special Collections, University of Calgary Library.

artifacts and structures in a natural setting so that visitors can enjoy strolling along the boardwalks, ride the train, visit the old Mounted Police post or the little church. The old-fashioned ice cream parlour is very popular, as is the dining room of the old hotel. Fresh bread can be bought at the bakery, its smell mingling with that of the sage growing wild. Film companies have used this authentic setting—among them, the CBC which produced the very successful television production about the Chautauqua, a romantic comedy set in a prairie town in the twenties.

The provincial government presented Calgarians with another gift, the Southern Alberta Jubilee Auditorium, by far the most sumptuous accommodation for stage and musical entertainment then available in the city, with generous seating, practice rooms and large foyers. It opened in 1957 with a production of *As You Like It*, with local actors in Jacobean costumes. This production immediately revealed the flaws in the conception of the facility, for the actors could not be heard unless they moved near the mikes

The official opening of the Glenbow Museum building in downtown Calgary, September 20, 1976. On the extreme left is Ralph Steinhauer, the first Indian to become Lieutenant-Governor of Alberta, and on the extreme right is Premier Peter Lougheed. Glenbow Museum.

concealed in the stage shrubbery. However, the beautiful building became home to the large membership of the Calgary Film Society and to the Calgary Philharmonic. It was available to an unending succession of travelling opera, ballet, and musical groups and musical comedy companies. The Calgary Philharmonic Orchestra, formed in 1955, prospered under distinguished and energetic conductors. As young professionals gradually replaced the amateur musicians, Calgarians became very proud of their orchestra.

Local theatre groups continued to perform in a variety of milieus, but in the middle sixties, two groups amalgamated with the name M.A.C. 14 Club, under the artistic direction of Ken Dyba. In its first year, the club produced a series of remarkable successes, including *The Knack*, directed by Joyce Doolittle and starring Sharon Pollock, which won at the Dominion Drama Festival. Doolittle had come to Calgary in 1961 with theatrical training and experience and startled audi-

"The Knack," starring, from left to right, Sharon Pollock, Robert Haley, James Eberle, and Michael Ball. Glenbow Archives/PA-15378 #1.

ences with her bawdy production of *Lysistrata* and her introduction of Beckett when she produced *Krapp's Last Tape*. In 1968, she directed a fine production of Beckett's *Happy Days,* which won at the provincial drama festival. She also worked successfully in drama with children at the Allied Arts Centre.

From the luxuriant growth of live theatre in Calgary, two main theatre companies eventually emerged: Theatre Calgary, a transformation by Christopher Newton of M.A.C. 14, and Alberta Theatre Projects (ATP). Theatre Calgary used the stage at the Allied Arts Centre, while ATP had a curious and modest beginning at Heritage Park under the direction of Douglas Riske and his wife, Paddy Campbell. She was the talented author of the children's plays they produced at the Allied Arts Centre theatre and also in the schools. At the old Canmore Opera House, which had been moved to Heritage Park, ATP produced a number of plays by local writers, such as John Murrell's *Waiting for the Parade*, Sharon Pollock's the *Wreck of the National Line Car,* and *The Devil's Instrument* by W.O. Mitchell. These writers and others were also represented in Theatre Calgary's programming, such as Sharon Pollock's *Walsh,* also produced at Stratford, and W.O. Mitchell's, *The Black Bonspiel of Willie MacCrimmon*.

The range of live theatre greatly expanded when the University of Alberta at Calgary gained its autonomy in 1966 and became The University of Calgary. It formed the first Faculty of Fine Arts in Canada and almost immediately offered excellent programs in drama, art, and music. Victor Mitchell headed the department of drama, which could use both the well-equipped University Theatre and the Reeve Theatre for rehearsal and experimental production.

Under the guidance of Mitchell and the creativity of the members of the faculty, the university presented a number of original and memorable performances of the classics and contemporary theatre.

Specialists in all aspects of music including composition staffed the music department. The department invited the public to concerts by such professors as pianist Marilyn Engle, or singer Alexander Gray, as well as to student recitals and performances by the student orchestra. Music was sometimes incorporated into dramatic performances, which frequently featured Professor Quenten Doolittle's compositions. Talman Hertz, cellist, organized Pro Musica, the very popular concert series, which featured touring chamber music groups performing in the University Theatre. When the Canadian Music Centre located its Prairie Regional Office at The University of Calgary in 1980, musicians had at their disposal scores and recordings of Canadian music, as well as the resources of The Violet Archer Library. To celebrate the 25th anniversary of the Centre, John Snow, with the cooperation of the Centre, arranged for a chamber music performance of the works of local composers. This proved so successful that New Works Calgary was established to organize programs of contemporary Canadian music, especially that of Alberta composers.

The Art Department offered studio courses in painting, printmaking, ceramics and sculpture, as well as art history and appreciation classes. The teaching staff included artists with national reputations, such as John Hall and Kenneth Esler. When the Nickle Arts Museum was donated to the university by another family who had profited by the oil industry, a proper exhibition space became available to graduating students and faculty.

The members of the English Department, many of whom were creative writers, such as Ian Adam or Christopher Wiseman, greatly enhanced the study and enjoyment of literature. They stimulated the creativity of their students and also played their part in literary circles outside the university. Wiseman was very active in poetry circles and James Black delighted both students and the public with his brilliant and infectious appreciation of Shakespeare. In the seventies, the university initiated a creative writing program involving such writers as Aritha van Herk and W.P. Kinsella, and the work of the graduates began to be published. Local literary magazines such as *The Blue Buffalo* and *The Dandelion* appeared and struggled into life. The university library provided an additional resource for the reading public to complement the rapidly expanding public library system.

Funds from the Canada Council, Alberta Culture and the Calgary Regional Arts Foundation in part nourished this cultural ferment. The Regional Arts Foundation administered by dedicated

Calgary Centre for Performing Arts about 1988. Calgary Centre for Performing Arts.

volunteers, was set up by the City of Calgary to provide money (at arms length) to a wide variety of cultural groups. The seventies proved a period of growth and consolidation, which underlay the exciting developments of the eighties which saw the construction of the Calgary Centre for Performing Arts. Under a committee established by the Calgary Regional Arts Foundation headed by a Calgary citizen, Martha Cohen, volunteers planned and raised money. Work began in 1981 on a centre that would house the Calgary Philharmonic, Theatre Calgary and Alberta Theatre Projects, and a variety of other performance activities. When the complex opened in 1985, it consisted of the Jack Singer Concert Hall, the Max Bell Theatre, and the Martha Cohen Theatre, with a full complement of auxiliary facilities.

Under the baton of Mario Bernardi, the Philharmonic tested the acoustics of the Singer Hall. They proved to be brilliant. At the gala opening, an eager audience watched Brian MacDonald's ballet for R. Murray Schafer's *Garden of the Heart* with Maureen Forrester as soloist. This evening was followed by a second devoted to Mahler's *Symphony #8* with soloists and choir under Bernardi's direction. Over the next years, the maestro raised the status of the orchestra to the highest standard. Orchestral playing flourished and Mount Royal College gained renown for its orchestras and numerous performing groups from choirs and chamber music and jazz ensembles.

The Calgary Centre for Performing Arts provides the theatre community with superb facilities. Theatre Calgary occupies the larger space with the Max Bell Theatre, while Alberta Theatre Projects plays in the Martha Cohen Theatre, which in design resembles European facilities with the audience close to the stage in sharply rising tiers. Theatre Calgary, more spacious and less flexible, has offered, under a series of directors, solid, well-performed plays of proven worth. ATP, under the dynamic direction of Michael Dobbin, a native-born Calgarian, has produced more experimental works.

With the 1988 Winter Olympics, Calgary took its place on the world stage. An Olympic Arts Festival was organized, which offered fine performances of Peter Brook's *Carmen* and Gershwin's *Porgy and Bess*, special art films were shown in local theatres, and art galleries mounted carefully curated exhibitions. Outstanding was *The Spirit Sings* at the Glenbow Museum, a collection of precious artifacts created by the Native peoples of Canada and assembled from all over the world. Superbly mounted, it was a tribute to the First Nations. Glenbow and the publishers McClelland and Stewart published a beautiful volume illustrating the exhibition.

Books and literature were celebrated when Mme Sauve presented the Governor General's Awards in Calgary to coincide with the opening of the Olympics. Citizens and visitors packed the Convention Centre anxious to hear various authors speak, to buy books at the booths and to enjoy the buzz of the literary world. Even the organizers were surprised at the enthusiasm of the crowds. But they should not have been—this is a booklovers' city. Calgarians borrowed from the public library the largest number of books per capita in Canada, and their school library system is one of the finest in the country. In 1988, children's librarians and teachers organized the fourth conference, Kaleidoscope, celebrating children's literature. This prestigious international conference held in Calgary attracts specialists from all over the continent and from Britain to discuss the work of authors and illustrators for children.

After the Olympics, the city continued to attract wide attention with international competitions and festivals ranging from the Calgary International Jazz Festival to the Calgary International Organ Festival. The first was initiated in 1980 outdoors on Prince's Island. It now flourishes for ten days every year. The second was inspired by the gift of a magnificent organ for the Singer Hall in memory of a local citizen, Margaret Mannix. Young organists from all over the world were invited to compete for a gold medal, a concert tour, a recording engagement and a $12,000 cash prize. An organ concerto, *Sno Walker* was commissioned from Michael Colgrass and played with the Calgary Philharmonic. The CBC's broadcast of the competition attracted large local audiences and generated new interest in organ music. Subsequently, free lunch-

47

time organ concerts were offered to the public and proved very popular.

The Esther Honens International Piano Competition was funded by the donor of the five-million-dollar endowment which enables the organizers to stage the event every four years. This competition for young musicians has several unusual features that ensure the continuing progress of the competitors. These conditions were put in place by the first artistic director, Calgary musician Gloria Saarinen. Hundreds of volunteers were involved over an eighteen-month period. The interest and public attendance at even the master classes given by the judges was astonishing.

The Banff International String Quartet Competition, another important competition, was first offered at the Banff School of Fine Arts in 1983. These young musicians attract keen audiences and their performances are broadcast over the CBC. Large numbers of Calgarians drive back and forth to Banff every summer to the now well-established Festival of Fine Arts, where they enjoy modern and classical opera, chamber music, ballet, jazz, drama, film, or lectures.

In 1993, the school celebrated its sixtieth anniversary, and notable among the events was the first annual conference on acoustic ecology, *The Tuning of the World,* inspired by the work of the composer R. Murray Schafer. The conference, coordinated by Tim Buell, composer and professor at The University of Calgary, attracted over two hundred delegates from all over the world. The Banff school had been under the stewardship of The University of Calgary since 1966, and the close cooperation has proved fruitful. To complement the conference, an intriguing exhibition of sound-based art was organized at the Nickle Art Museum using tapes and video screens. *My Mother's Living Room* by Robert Hamilton shows his mother playing popular songs on an electronic instrument, which comically continues playing without the mother's touch. *Acoustic Line as the Crow Listens* by Steve Heimbecker offers four soundscapes at Calgary locations. The arts of film and video have flourished in the eighties, and the video productions of Calgarian Leila Sujir have been shown nationally and abroad.

The facilities and personnel for making films and the landscape around the city have attracted numerous film crews from all over the continent. Les Kimber, a graduate of Betty Mitchell's Workshop 14, has been involved in such films as *Little Big Man* and *Don't Shoot the Teacher* and was recognized in 1993 for his thirty-year contribution to Alberta's film industry. Douglas Berquist of Calgary is in the process of shooting his film of Sharon Pollock's powerful play *Death in the Family,* starring the author herself.

Canadian and international videos shown at night in the Olympic Plaza were a feature of the 1993 Art Week, a September event, which brings art and architecture out into public view. Calgary architects designed bird houses, which were hung in Tomkins Park and later auctioned. The noted Calgary artists who painted the colourful murals on the buildings along 17th Avenue SW, one of the main arteries of the city, answered questions about their work. All the art galleries featured special exhibitions, and the largest assemblage, *Abstraction: Which Way from Here,* comprised over 200 works by Canadian and famous international artists. Dr. John Polanyi, one of Canada's Nobel Prize Winners, spoke on the creative thinking common to both artists and scientists.

Another famous Canadian, writer Michael Ondaatje, spoke at the initiation of the Markin-Flanagan Distinguished Writers Programme at The University of Calgary. A generous donation enables the university to bring to Calgary every year a writer of international status and to fund a writer-in-residence program. This gift enriches the creative writing program, which has already resulted in the publication of novels, stories, and poetry by local writers.

As the city celebrates its hundredth birthday, its citizens enjoy a wealth of cultural opportunities, the result of the initiatives of dedicated individual citizens, nourished by generous gifts and public funds. Alberta Culture added the term "Multiculturalism" to its title in the late 1980s, reflecting the demographic changes of recent years[1]; changes which have resulted in the influence of Asian and African immigrants being brought to bear on the predominantly American and European sources of the city's culture. No doubt from this rich mix will emerge a new and even more exciting Calgary.

Note

[1] Recently, the name has been changed again to "Alberta Community Development."

Adjustment and Leadership: Women in Calgary

Janice Dickin McGinnis

The story of women in Calgary is one of adjustment and leadership. Overwhelmingly from "away," women in this community of accelerating growth and fierce ambition have established lives not only for themselves and those under their care but also for the city itself. They continue to carry their load in support of the agendas of others and, with the decrease over the last few decades in gender-specific discrimination, have moved into previously proscribed areas of achievement and service. Established at the end of one century, Calgary at the end of another finds itself faced with a new set of challenges. We are on a new frontier in which the importance of the leadership of women—

more than at any other time in recorded history—is being openly recognized. What roles they choose and how well they fill them will have fundamental effects on the future of Calgary and Calgarians.

There were, of course, women here before Calgary existed. Native women created and cared for their families and their communities, providing food, clothing, comfort and a significant part of the cultural life. Arguably, the lives of these women and of the settler women who came later formed more of a continuum than did the lives of their men. Women were charged with the maintenance of private life, looking to the bodily and psychological needs of men and children and then themselves, needs essentially the same no matter what economic and political systems are in place.

So, in some respects, it is possible to argue that Native women were less affected by settlement onto reserves than were their menfolk. While Native men saw a large part of their roles as hunters made redundant with the disappearance by 1879 of the buffalo from the Canadian side of the border, Na-

Two women gained election to the Calgary City Council in 1950: Rose Wilkinson (front row, third from the left) and Mary Dover (front row, fourth from the left). Glenbow Archives/NA-2864-922a.

tive women, by and large, still knew what they had to do when they got up each morning. Somehow people had to be fed, clothed and sheltered. In addition, there was the precious art of teaching a culture to be practised. Daily, these women faced the uphill battle of preserving old ways in the face of destruction, displacement, and the demoralization they inevitably entail.

The dignity that such women maintained can be found in descriptions such as Maria Campbell's of her "Cheechum," the Cree great-grandmother who served as anchor to descendants unable to evade the stresses and allures of modern life.[1] We have much to learn from these women. Providing domestic stability in the face of vastly changed circumstances is a challenge Calgary women have continued to face, even down to the immigrants of today.

Some Native women did not choose to try to carry the torch of their birth culture: instead, they sought a place for themselves among the conquerors. It has been argued that Native women had both opportunities and reasons to assimilate that were not shared by their brothers.[2] Early in the history of Calgary, Native and Metis women were pressed into the service of men. One need was for dance partners. At its inaugural Christmas dinner in 1875, the fort provided dinner for those living nearby. Dancing, with Metis women for partners, followed.[3]

Women were also sought to fill other roles. Native prostitutes were not uncommon, but neither were Native wives. White men on the frontier had contracted both "legal" and common law forms of marriage with Native women for centuries. Some of the descendants of these women had by this point been fully assimilated by white society. One such was Isabella Christine Hardisty, eastern-educated and related at one and the same time to Lady Strathcona and to west coast Natives. She would marry James Alexander Lougheed, senator and Sir, with whom she would establish one of Calgary's great turn-of-the-century mansions.

In the less elevated echelons of Calgary society, wiving was also a preoccupation. The Mounties, for instance, were out not only to get their man but also their "woman." While some found partners among women of the West, others went home on leave to marry sweethearts, and still others entered into mutual agreements to bring out female relatives for one another's inspection.[4] In the racially conscious atmosphere of Western Canada in the late nineteenth century, there can be no doubt that the preferred wives of white men were white women.[5]

To be fair, it was not simply racial purity these men, and later women, wished to prescribe for the new settlement but cultural continuity. People may leave home for a variety of reasons, but immigrant fantasy encompasses the dream of bringing a great deal of home with you. That is not always possible, but the possibility increases directly in proportion to the size and homogeneity of the group in question and the "emptiness" of the area moved into. The job of the Mounties in "emptying" the land having been accomplished, it was now possible to fill it with a model of what had been left behind. It is women who keep a culture going, from food to religion, from clothing to recitals, from outhouses to education. If you wanted "white" culture, you needed white women. It was that simple.

These women had a big job ahead of them. First of all, they were a distinct minority. Even so late as 1911, the ratio of single men to single women was still roughly three to two (26,565 to 17,139). This faced "respectable" married women not only with what must have seemed the insurmountable job of civilizing all these bachelors, but also with special problems in providing what would have been viewed as the normal amount of care for their families. Then, out of all proportion to our experience now, middle-class women depended on domestic help. Families were larger, houses harder to clean, food less "convenient." Fabrics were anything but "easy care" and, in a town of more mud, more physical labour and fewer baths, laundry took up the entire Monday of every week. Women aspiring to a genteel manner of living for their families and a modicum of leisure for themselves *needed* domestic help. Like Mounties seeking wives, housewives seeking maids imported them from back home, only to see them become wives themselves in short order.[6]

This was, of course, a victory as well as a defeat. In addition to their onerous domestic duties, respectable women were supposed to set the style for a respectable town. Respectable towns by the definition of the times were made up of nuclear families, not of boarding houses and brothels, the other havens available for single men looking for the services and solace of women. Certainly respectable women with the time and inclination for political work early chose to adopt issues that could be depicted as direct threats to the "family." One was prostitution: "respectable" women saw "working girls" as threats to city-building, not as sisters in the struggle. Another was alcohol: women campaigned for the right to vote (granted provincially in 1916, federally in 1918) on a platform of moral reform, heavily dependent on the social gains claimed for prohibition.

The basic acceptable argument for female suffrage was that women should have the vote because they were "purer" than men and were needed to make decisions that would ensure survival of the family and of what was basically the anglo-Canadian middle-class way of life so prized by themselves and the country's economic and political elites. Racial overtones also accompanied the arguments of the suffragists: "foreign" men had the vote, while anglo-Canadian women did not. Suffragists considered this not only unfair but dangerous.

Alberta women were heavily involved in the struggle for women's suffrage. Among them was Nellie McClung, one of the "Famous Five" Alberta women who would succeed in 1929 in having Canadian women declared "persons" (and therefore eligible for a variety of legal rights) by Britain's Privy Council after Canada's own Supreme Court refused to grant them that status. A house McClung lived in during the 1920s still stands at the corner of 15 Avenue and 7 Street SW.

It is not always easy now to feel sisterhood for Calgary's early "City Mothers." They were spokeswomen for their sex but also for their class and their culture. The reforms they envisioned were meant to remove what they saw as impediments to the sort of life they aspired to. They sought to establish a certain way of life, one to which they meant white immigrant groups to aspire and all other immigrant groups to support from a respectful distance. These women would have been alarmed by the current racial make-up of our city and stunned by the idea of state-supported multiculturalism.

But it would be silly to reject them for their faults rather than to celebrate their very real attributes. Women reformers fought long and hard and often successfully to improve the quality of life in this little community. Of grave concern was the question of public health. If one wants to build a city, one had best guard against disease, which kills off population. One had also better assure

Waiting room, Victorian Order of Nurses baby clinic, Calgary, between 1911 and 1914. Glenbow Archives/NA-1068-3.

natural increase by caring for children and the women who bear them. Reform initiatives in these areas depended largely on the motivation of women who could and chose to take on a job extra to their already extensive home-making chores.

A variety of ways exist in which women can clothe themselves with power. One is simply to work on the titular head of the family group for the changes one cannot publicly work for oneself. Another is to work long hours behind the scenes doing good works that are unlikely to get done on any official level: women's efforts in this manner have been particularly encouraged in the areas of volunteer social work, often done through organized religion, and cultural work, often accomplished through amateur arts organizations. Certainly Calgary women who chose these routes made a tremendous difference to the life of the city. Kathleen Snow's chapter on cultural life demonstrates how female-driven much of this work was. Another example of a woman who successfully wielded the power to change conditions through "non-political" means was Mrs. Harold W. Riley, who laboured long in the fields of "child and family welfare" and who was referred to on at least one occasion as "a plump little tyrant."[7]

Other women chose to take the chance suffrage granted them of wielding power openly and in their own names. Nellie McClung was one, serving as a Member of the Legislative Assembly in the 1920s. Less well-known is Annie Gale, who served as Calgary's first alderwoman from 1918 to 1925. A veteran of the struggle to provide better and cheaper food supplies for Calgary housewives during the Great War, Gale concentrated much of her energy during her years in office on the issue of public health.[8] Among other things, she supported public clinics for children and pushed for better care for women in childbirth. Sharply pointing out that the priorities of male community-builders do not always encompass the priorities of female ones, she charged that: "While the government provides a veterinary surgeon free of charge, or for a nominal fee of $1, to attend the delivery of a foal, women have their babies unattended."[9]

In the arena of infant and maternal mortality, suffragettes like Gale found common cause with "City Mothers" like Riley. In truth, Calgary's infant mortality rate was appalling, as was Alberta's and all of Canada's, for that matter. In 1911, Calgary lost over 100 infants for every 1,000 born, more than half of these within the first month of life.

The high mortality rate was due to a variety of factors. Babies born in winter had to survive the erratic heating of even the best houses. Babies born in summer were susceptible to diarrhea, not then treatable by drugs and procedures (e.g. in-

Home economics class at King George School, about 1912 or earlier. Glenbow Archives/NA-5063-1.

travenous introduction of fluids) now readily available to us. And then there were the so-called childhood diseases, not just measles and mumps but scarlet fever, whooping cough and a whole host of other ailments now held in check through public health programs. Even simple sores and infections that mothers feel only mild alarm at discovering today could cause death in the age before antibiotics.

Who nursed these children? Who stayed up all night? Who was responsible for finding out and concocting necessary treatments, doing whatever was possible? In most cases, it was a mother with other young children, already bearing heavy responsibilities to her husband and her house, and often carrying another child at the same time. One of the reasons then for the high infant mortality rate was not just what happened to the child after birth but tenuous health on the part of the mother during pregnancy. Calgary women had many more babies then than we do now. Some had them until their bodies wore out from it. Not surprisingly, the maternal mortality rate was also high.

Partly, women had more children then as a matter of social policy. Even Nellie McClung managed five, despite her heavy political work. A community seeking to increase its population has a stake in encouraging its women to reproduce. Limitation of family size was publicly denounced as "race suicide." The idea of "the family" as the building block of society served to encourage even women who had access to birth control to opt for more than one or two children. But the truth was that many women had access neither to birth control nor to the basic information on reproduction now taught to children in elementary school. It was, in fact, a criminal offence in Canada until 1969 to disseminate birth control information. Doctors did not always choose to break this law.

We know that women were often desperate to limit their family size. Unaware that they were asking someone to break the law, they wrote heart-rending pleas to such publications as The Western Producer: "I am 31, the mother of 7 children, eldest 11 years, and youngest 8 months, not at all strong, and owing to farm conditions, very heavily in debt. I would like to have any information I can get re birth control."

The women's columnist for the Producer, Violet McNaughton, could not reply in print. To do so would have been to risk being charged for "corrupting public morals" under the obscenity section of the Criminal Code. She did, however, sometimes risk reply in private, sending women a recipe for what were called "prairie brownies," half-inch fudge-like cubes made of cocoa butter and laced with boric and tannic acid, to be inserted into the vagina.[10] Body heat would melt the brownie into a shield across the mouth of the cervix thereby functioning as a barrier. While it is true that McNaughton wrote from Saskatchewan and that the main readership of the Producer was rural Western Canada, few Calgary women knew of these or similar methods.

In fact, if one were to characterize the role of women in the building of Calgary, it would be as that of "helpers." By and large they would be happy with that role until it began to lose status drastically after the Second World War. Once that happened, women insisted upon entering more public arenas, on shifting their leadership more into the open. In the interim, they carried the burden for the "invisible" aspects of daily life: the under-recognized if not entirely unrecognized contributions of the arts and sciences necessary to living lives. They also found themselves rushed into service in "emergencies."

Traditionally, it is women who have cared not only for the young and the old but also for the sick of all ages. We have little concept now, with our drugs and our institutions and our higher standard of health, of just how heavy a burden that could be. Diseases we do not even think about anymore, such as tuberculosis, involved intensive nursing care on the part of our grandmothers and even mothers. Epidemics, the most notable one being the influenza epidemic of 1918-19, saw women pressed into service. Women also bore much of the burden during the economic downturn of the 1930s.

Another perceived emergency, and one that would in many ways spawn the modern feminist movement, was the Second World War.

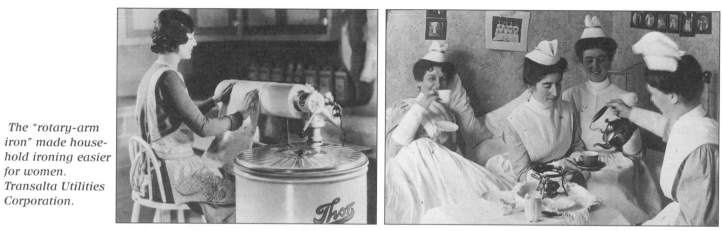

The "rotary-arm iron" made household ironing easier for women. Transalta Utilities Corporation.

Tea time for nurses, Calgary General Hospital, 1904. Glenbow Archives/ NA-2600-3.

Stenographer pool, land department, CPR Department of Natural Resources, 1915. Glenbow Archives/NA-5055-1.

A Calgary woman in her kitchen, April 1958. Glenbow Archives/ NC-60-16.

Women had also been called on to help out in the First World War, and they had demanded suffrage in return for service. They again felt entitled to change in return for extensive service during this second conflict. While Calgary women had been moving into what economists define as the work force as teachers, nurses, secretaries, librarians, waitresses, salesgirls, factory workers, and so on for quite some time, the general expectation was that if one married, one stopped work. But not during wartime. Partly women could handle a double role because families had become smaller. Availability of new labour-saving devices was also a factor. In addition, a simple lowering of standards in food preparation and housework saved women hours, while seemingly having no harmful effects on family health.

At least that was the accepted belief until the men came marching home. The 1950s saw a re-deification of the family and pressures to make that once again women's full-time concern. Some women no doubt welcomed this return to what for them was normal. Others put their excess energy back into the unpaid labour of "good works." Women wishing to continue in their jobs sometimes found themselves actively barred from employment (for example with the City of Calgary) if they were married.

The war gave women a taste of their own strength and their ability to adapt. It also taught them that they could do "men's work" without sacrificing feminine principles, something they had been warned for decades would happen if they took work outside the home. They could also see that, for all the lip service paid to it, the work of caring for husband, home, and children offered little real status or power in the post-war rush towards prosperity. The daughters who came of age in the sixties fought for the right of women to a place in the business and professional worlds.

A mark of the success of this movement in opening doors for women can be found in the ratio of female to male students enrolled full-time at The University of Calgary. During the academic year 1969-70, women already comprised more than one third of the full-time students. By 1992-93, they comprised more than half. In addition, many women—often the heads of single parent families—still choose to study part-time.

Some of these women at the university are daughters of daughters of the city, but increasingly they are the daughters of women displaced from other lands, from other lives. These women have come to their own frontier in a post-modern city which has begun to fulfil its early ambitions for sophistication and national, if not international, status. Like others before them, they will learn to adjust. One has only to look at a book like *Homes in Alberta*[11] to gain some appreciation of the changes women have been asked to go through in the short history of non-Native population in this part of the world. There is much yet to be known about these women. Although it has made great strides in recent years, women's history is still largely undone. This leaves the spotlight to men, by default. But lack of attention should never be confused with lack of importance. Norman Macleod, son of Mary Isabella Drever Macleod who came to what is now southern Alberta in the mid-1870s with her husband, the Colonel, would agree with this. Norman said in later life: "Ninety percent of the hardship in the west was suffered by the women. Men could get away from the hardship but women were always face to face with it."[12]

Women still struggle against hardship in this city. It is in that struggle that they find best expression of their capacity for leadership. We are currently told by our politicians and economists that we are all on a new frontier. How well this city deals with that will be in large part in the hands of our women.

Notes

[1] Maria Campbell, *Halfbreed* (Toronto: Seal Books, 1973). While this book is not Calgary-specific, it remains the best source regarding the difficulties of transition for Western Canadian Native women in our culture.

[2] See Sylvia van Kirk, *Many Tender Ties. Women in Fur-Trade Society in Western Canada, 1670-1870* (Winnipeg: Watson and Dwyer, 1980).

[3] Lawrence H. Bussard, "Early History of Calgary" (unpublished M.A. thesis, University of Alberta, 1935), p. 27.

[4] Joy Duncan, "They Also Served," in *Red Serge Wives*, edited by Wilma Clevette et al. (Edmonton: Lone Pine Publishing, 1985), pp. 17-22.

[5] Sarah Carter, "Categories and Terrains of Exclusion. Constructing the "Indian Woman" in the Early Settlement Era in Western Canada" *Great Plains Quarterly* 13 (Summer 1993), 147-161.

[6] Catherine Philip, "The Fair, Frail Flowers of Western Womanhood", in *Frontier Calgary. Town, City and Region, 1875-1914*, edited by A. W. Rasporich and Henry Klassen (Calgary: McClelland and Stewart West, 1975), p. 115.

[7] Elise A. Corbet, "A. Maude Riley. A Do-Gooder, Not a Suffragette," in *Citymakers: Calgarians after the Frontier*, edited by Max Foran and Sheilagh S. Jameson (Calgary: Historical Society of Alberta, Chinook Country Chapter, 1987), p. 209.

[8] Heather Foran, "Annie Gale. Reformer, Feminist and First Woman Alderman in Calgary," in *Citymakers*, pp. 197-207.

[9] Annie Gale, quoted in Elise Corbet, "Alberta Women in the 1920's" (M.A. thesis, University of Calgary, 1979), p. 90.

[10] Mrs. E.J.M., *The Western Producer*, 29 Sept. 1927 and typescript from McNaughton's personal papers, in Linda Rasmussen et al., *A Harvest Yet to Reap. A History of Prairie Women* (Toronto: The Women's Press, 1976), p. 72.

[11] Donald G. Wetherell and Irene R.A. Knet, *Homes in Alberta: Building, Trends, and Design* (Edmonton: University of Alberta Press, 1991).

[12] Quoted in Duncan, supra, p. 29.

Community Participation and Civic Spirit

Roger Gibbins and Harry H. Hiller

When Canadians try to describe their cities, they have a number of options from which to choose. Some will select the physical characteristics of their community, highlighting such things as the green foliage and rain forest of Vancouver, or the rocky coastal terrain of St. John's. Others may draw more upon their city's historical significance and emphasize its structural features; for example, the Citadel in Halifax or the rich, historical past reflected in the older parts of Quebec City. Still others may stress their community's cultural life, its cosmopolitan diversity, its climate (particularly people living in Victoria), or even the record of its professional sports teams. In this last respect, both Edmonton—"the city of champions"—and Toronto—"home of the Blue Jays!"—come readily to mind. All of these images represent means whereby city residents come to define their communities.

Although Calgarians also quickly draw attention to their city's physical environment and professional teams, and to climatic features such as the chinooks, they have generally adopted a different strategy of civic identification. In part, they have done so because Calgary has a somewhat ambiguous geographic location. Is Calgary truly a "prairie" city as it is often assumed? The city sits where the prairies end and the foothills begin; the land begins to buckle almost as soon as one crosses Centre Street heading west. While Calgary has the highest elevation of any Canadian city, Calgary is not quite a prairie or mountain city; it lacks the unambiguous terrain of a Winnipeg ("Gateway to the prairie West") or Denver ("mile high city"). Nor are many of its geographic landmarks of such prominence that they could be used to project a memorable image of Calgary for a national or international audience. Calgary is known more for its proximity to Banff and the Rockies than for its own features such as Fish Creek, the Bow River Valley, or the Glenmore Reservoir.

If its physical setting or historical significance are not the key features of Calgary, then what is it that gives our city its character? The civic identity most strongly conveyed to the outside world is its distinctive community spirit. The image may be somewhat contrived and may not always correspond to reality, but it remains a powerful image nonetheless. And in that sense, the image helps produce action and behaviour that reinforces expectations. While Calgarians are justifiably proud of their city's physical environment, cultural endowments, and growing social diversity, what is used time and time again to set Calgary apart from other cities in Canada and North America is its robust civic spirit.

In this chapter, we want to make a number of relatively straightforward but nonetheless important points: first, to establish that Calgarians' self-perceptions are in fact well-founded; second, to explain why this civic spirit exists; third, to show that it reveals some important things about the kinds of people we are, and the kind of community in which we live.

The Calgary Civic Spirit

Calgary's civic spirit has its roots in the myths of the western frontier. It has been perpetuated through high profile events such as the annual Stampede, the Olympics, and more broadly based volunteer activity.

At the heart of Calgary's character is its "western" image. Other cities have acted as service centres to a surrounding agricultural community, but no Canadian city has used that background to support its image and mythologies like Calgary. Not only has the white Stetson become a marketing symbol, but it also reflects an urbane accommodation to that rural background that all Calgarians

Woman pricing hats at Lammles Western Wear booth in the Big Four building at the Stampede, late June 1991. Calgary Sun, June 26, 1991.

Governor General Vincent Massey (second from the left) at the Calgary Rotary Club's mammoth Stampede Barbecue at Mewata Park, July 1958. Glenbow Archives/NA-2864-1086.

can identify with. (Even children have their own white Stetsons to wear at appropriate occasions!) While Calgarians did not invent the "Ya-hoo" yell, all Calgarians recognize it as our own way of celebrating. This selective adaptation of our agricultural past helps distinguish Calgary from other cities and provides key symbols to our civic spirit.

This frontier agricultural background also provides the events that promote that distinctive identity. Chuckwagon breakfasts and western barbecues transform a simple meal into a time of fun and friendship and an expression of hospitality, whether for locals or for visitors.

The most internationally distinctive event is the annual July whoop-up known as the Calgary Stampede. The idea of an agricultural fair is common to many cities. However, Calgary has transformed it into a giant party. A nationally televised parade and rodeo events combined with chuckwagon races in front of thousands of tourists provide activities unknown in other major cities. Normal business

In 1948, the Calgary Stampeders won the Grey Cup by beating Ottawa 12-7 in Toronto. This crowd gathered downtown to welcome home their conquering heroes. Calgary Herald photo. Glenbow Archives/NA-2864-13288A.

activity slows down during Stampede as "urban cowboys" dress western and retailers transform the appearance of their establishments into frontier outposts.

Calgarians have transferred the symbols of their Stampede and urban "trademarks" to other contexts as well. The face of the Grey Cup, for instance, was changed in 1948 when the Calgary Stampeders participated in the national football final. The Stampede spirit, including chuckwagon breakfast and horses, even in the lobby of Toronto's Royal York Hotel, went far beyond the football field. When Calgary hosted the 1988 Winter Olympic Games, it sponsored a giant chuckwagon breakfast before the opening ceremonies. Similarly, whenever conventions are held in the city, a chuckwagon breakfast is automatically expected.

Central to our civic spirit, these frontier western-based events help Calgarians develop a clear sense of who "we" are. They instil civic pride and provide an opportunity for relaxation and fun. They also enable us to export our identity nationally and internationally in a distinctive way. The central message behind it all is one of cordiality and hospitality. Chuckwagon breakfasts, for example, are almost always free. Shopping malls serve thousands of office breakfasts every July. Guests are always shown a good time. The event creates a spirit of warmth and good feelings that break down the expressions of reserve and distance normally associated with urban living. While other cities have their own annual festivals, none of their events are so tightly linked to their urban identity. Furthermore, whereas urban life is often seen as distant and formal, such perceptions are offset in Calgary by the openness, warmth, and friendliness of the Stampede spirit.

What other evidence can we find for a unique community spirit in Calgary? Perhaps the most high profile event ever hosted by the city was the 1988 Winter Olympic Games. In typical Calgary fashion, the community transformed the athletic event into an urban festival. The Olympic theme song with its refrain: "Can't you feel it the spirit surrounds you. Can't you feel it now that it found you. Can't you feel it now that its everywhere. Can't you feel it here," capti-

The 1988 Winter Olympics opening at McMahon Stadium. Calgary Sun.

vated the Olympics as a feeling and a community spirit rather than just an event. Calgary adopted the weak performers, such as Eddie the Eagle and the Jamaican Bobsled Team. Pin trading reached a feverish pitch and the neighbourhood pageantry program encouraged local homes to be suitably decorated for the occasion. The role of the downtown Olympic Plaza and its nightly laser show and medal ceremonies provided a significant event in which all citizens could participate—even without tickets. The Eighth Avenue Mall came alive on a daily basis with entertainers and general milling to create a spirit of excitement. For many people, it was not what was happening at the competition sites that was important but what was happening downtown.

The high rate of community participation also made the Calgary Olympics distinctive. While official Olympic volunteers numbered about 9,400, thousands of other citizens volunteered in other capacities. For example, 6,000 children and adults participated in the Opening Ceremonies, 2,000 volunteers sewed the required costumes, and several hundred high school students helped maintain the Saddledome between events. Even an Adopt-A-Parent program was established to provide lodging in local homes for parents of Olympic athletes. In a very real sense, the Olympics mobilized the community's civic spirit to an unprecedented level.

Alberta has the highest rate of volunteerism in the country. Calgary itself is usually thought to have the highest rate of volunteerism among Canada's major cities, due in part to special events like the annual Stampede and the 1988 Winter Olympics. However, the scope of volunteerism reaches well beyond such special events; it is characteristic of the city's social fabric. Four out of ten persons over fifteen years of age formally serve as volunteers in the city, a number that rises to seven out of ten when one also considers informal volunteers. In 1993, 34,600 persons responded to ads placed by the Calgary Volunteer Centre for persons looking for new volunteer positions. As has been said, "volunteerism is a motherhood issue" in Calgary. Even corporations support volunteering through the Calgary Corporate Volunteer Council.

A special aspect of volunteering and community participation is expressed in Calgary's 124 community associations, most of which possess their own buildings. Community associations are particularly strong in the West, compared to other parts of Canada, but Calgary joins Edmonton in possessing especially robust community associations. Not just social and sports entities, they exist to address community needs in everything from after-school care to urban planning and transportation needs.

Explaining Calgary's Civic Spirit

Some explain Calgary's civic spirit as a creation of the city's elite. Civic boosters, from this perspective, are those who profit from the image of a dynamic and friendly city. Although elites do play a role in fostering the civic spirit, there are, however, other important factors at play.

Calgary has a comparatively large proportion of its population who are well-educated middle-class people and middle-class people are more likely to be oriented towards community participation. Calgary is second only to Ottawa in terms of the percentage of the population holding a university degree. Conversely, of all major Canadian cities, Calgary has the lowest percentage of population with less than a Grade 9 education. Similarly, the average household income is the highest of all major Canadian Census Metropolitan Areas. While averages mask the extremes of the highs and the lows, there is substance to the white-collar professional image of Calgary. Perhaps most important is that white-collar professionals not only view volunteering and community participation as a pleasant outlet for their leisure time, but also are in positions where they can mobilize their employers to support community projects.

A second explanation for our robust community spirit can be found in the free-enterprise mentality that pervades the city. Our two dominant industries, agriculture and oil/gas, support a risk-taking ethic where individual effort and a venturesome spirit encourage rigorous and inten-

Danny Copithorne, President-elect and Steve Edwards (on the right), new General Manager, unveil the 1993 Stampede poster. Calgary Sun, May 30, 1993.

sive personal activity. Yet this world view is also counterbalanced by the frontier spirit of pulling together. It is ironic amidst this free-enterprise spirit that Calgary should possess the largest urban cooperative retailer in the world. This unique blend of "small town" thinking and adventurous risk-taking, amidst energy cycles of boom and bust, creates a special civic spirit not found in other Canadian cities.

The third explanation for our unique civic spirit relates to the size of our city. In 1951, our population was only around 125,000 and, in spite of enormous growth through the sixties and seventies, the city's population is still only about three-quarters of a million people—a far cry from most large metropolitan cities of several million. The significant high-rise office towers of the downtown, a rapid-transit system, and a large international airport give the appearance of a big city, yet the small-town culture still survives.

The dynamic growth which Calgary experienced, especially in the seventies, primarily resulted from in-migration from elsewhere in Canada and overseas. New residents eagerly sought to find their place in the new city which encouraged more citizen participation, and the population size of their newly adopted home was not foreboding to their involvement. The symbols discussed earlier provided warmer feelings of friendliness. Earlier migrants from surrounding rural areas brought their own notions of small-town participation with them.

Therefore, in a rather small city experiencing recent development and expansion, and aspiring for acceptance and recognition, civic pride finds it outlets in matters that carry this message. Thus the Stampede is not just a rodeo but also "the greatest outdoor show on earth," and the Olympics represented an opportunity to "tell the world" about a city on the grow.

What the Civic Spirit Says about Us as a Community

As previously noted, the chuckwagon breakfast defines the Calgary civic spirit and brings it to life. When visitors arrive during Stampede week, one of the traditions we share is to take them to a chuckwagon breakfast. Indeed, this event has become so popular that its use extends well beyond the Stampede. The Alberta Progressive Conservative Party's annual convention, for example, features a chuckwagon-style breakfast in which the Premier and cabinet ministers cook breakfast for convention delegates. When the Reform Party was attempting to establish a new presence and style on Parliament Hill, they drew from Calgary tradition and prepared a chuckwagon breakfast for Reform and Bloc Québécois MPs. (The Bloc brought the maple syrup!)

What does the chuckwagon breakfast reveal about the community and Calgarians? First, it removes boundaries and barriers. Although a particular community or group may sponsor and hold a breakfast in a particular location, the underlying assumption remains that it is open to all guests at no charge. It is, by design, an inclusive rather than exclusive event. It is also one open to all, regardless of age—a family event *par excellence*.

Second, the breakfast is a levelling event. It is something that anyone can cook, and indeed everyone does cook. It requires no lessons, no special knowledge or skill. The breakfast is also levelling in another way in that the community "elites" often do the cooking, a stylistic feature picked up nicely by the Progressive Conservative breakfast noted above. And finally, it is levelling across the gender divide; the breakfast is usually one that men cook and serve. It does not tax the gastronomic skills of even the most amateur cook and is also a very easy meal to clean up after.

Third, the breakfast stresses informality. Nobody dresses up, apart from digging out one's Stampede costume from the closet. No speeches, no head table, sometimes there is no table at all, as people sit on the curb or lawn chairs they have brought to the event. Finally, and by no means of least importance, the chuckwagon breakfast captures a "western" image that draws in turn from a long tradition of regional alienation. The chuckwagon breakfast is

Stampede breakfasts. Photos from The Calgary Sun.

everything that "the sophisticated East," of western Canadian mythology, is not: inclusive, levelling, informal, and casual.

Regardless of where and when it is held, the chuckwagon breakfast nicely captures the civic spirit that we have been discussing in this chapter. It breaks down the real barriers that normally exist between residents of a city to sustain the image of openness and friendliness. More than a symbol, the breakfast puts the civic spirit into action, puts it on display for the world to see.

The image of this civic spirit suggests an ideal about what Calgarians would like urban life to be. That the reality may often deviate from the ideal is less important than the fact that the image helps to humanize our urban environment and make it a particularly pleasant place in which to live.

The Future in Light of the Past

Grant MacEwan

The title is a subtle way of repeating the point that public planners need, and should possess, a good grasp of local history. Those qualified to offer guidance for tomorrow must be familiar with what happened yesterday. While tomorrow might not be an exact repetition of yesterday, the past might well suggest avenues to follow, or to avoid, in the future.

The western pioneers in community building spent little or no time searching local history for useful warnings and guidance, largely because there was no written local history. The railroad companies simply selected town sites eight or nine miles apart and demanded little more than good natural drainage. It was a simple matter. In most cases there was no serious thought at all to the probable quality of life or livability in the emerging towns or cities.

One may ponder the civic goals of Calgary's first mayor, George Murdoch, and the town's first and best pioneer builder, Major James Walker. They hoped for a school—any kind of school—a hospital, plank sidewalks, and an agricultural society capable of producing a good fair. For the broader community, they probably thought of nothing but settlers in numbers and taxpayers—any settlers or any taxpayers.

By the time Calgary became the area's first city in 1894, the priorities had changed only a little and included rapid population growth, railroad construction, and the consolidation of Calgary's place as a major distributing centre. The citymakers desired to make Calgary the new agricultural centre flourishing around the best agricultural fair west of Brandon, and to promote Calgary's sandstone for building purposes.

Still, the Calgary pattern was moderately conventional—until the pre-World War I real estate boom. The bust in 1913 left many bankruptcies, a corresponding number of financial survivors, and a Calgary with a strong addiction to booms. To bring comfort to those depressed real estate traders, the discovery of oil at Turner Valley in 1914 re-introduced the boom fever. Until a much bigger discovery of oil at Leduc, the Turner Valley demonstration was magnificent, and, happily for the city businessmen, it was in Calgary's backyard.

For the next twenty-five years any investors wishing to become part of the Turner Valley operations opened an office in Calgary. When Leduc, 175 miles to the north, burst upon the scene in 1947, most companies appeared satisfied to keep their offices in Calgary, and the southern city enjoyed a long series of oil booms until Calgarians looked upon them as their right by inheritance.

The Calgary oil interests prospered until it was declared, without proof, that Calgary had more oil-made millionaires per thousand of population than any other city on the continent. Nobody was much concerned about the possibility of the claim being false.

But while Calgary reaped the rewards of a rich new resource it did so complacently, for there was an obvious lack of balance in

Calgary's programme of industry. The city had difficulty in achieving the diversification that would have made the local economy more stable and more secure. "As long as you rely so heavily on oil and gas, you are in greater danger of suffering from the ups and downs and whims of the business world," Calgary was told. It was a fair warning. The proof came with the collapse of oil prices and the ongoing recession that many say will last for the rest of the century. Another criticism held that Calgary has been less enthusiastic about developing a strong and lively cultural life than it has been with oil and gas, Stampedes, and hockey.

The above criticisms notwithstanding, it does seem that a special variety of pioneer fibre and spirit was ever present in Calgary, and that frontier characteristics are still manifest. As the Calgary volunteer organizations can back with figures from a recent survey of volunteer services in cities Canada-wide, Calgary recorded more hours of volunteer service per thousand of population than any other city in Canada. Drawing upon pioneer spirit and co-operation, Calgary is still capable of being inspired to perform gigantic service. It further explains the spectacular success of Calgarians working without tangible reward when challenged by the hosting of the Olympic Winter Games. Calgarians showed they could do their city proud in the first Stampede of 1912; they did the same thing in 1988.

The future will see Calgarians with the spirit of James Walker and George Murdoch looking for a new area of service. It might well be an organized annual tour of historic show pieces within the province or country for that matter. Given our crucial need to develop a more environmentally conscious society Calgary might well draw on its pioneer spirit to give leadership to initiating and developing a continent-wide walking, biking, hiking trail beginning at Port Royal in Nova Scotia and ending at Fort Victoria in British Columbia. Its potential would be great. Such a grand scheme would need a tremendous level of commitment, but so did the Winter Olympics. It would be another test of the pioneer qualities of fibre and imagination that has characterized Calgary, and a dedication to the men and women of those early years and visible proof of their enduring legacy.

Calgarians have shown the same brand of pioneer spirit and tenacity over the past hundred years in both good times and bad. The city has always met its challenges head on and successfully. Now that it has grown to maturity Calgary must turn its face to a world less fortunate, to people still lacking in the basic necessities of life. The Calgarian of the future may have to draw more deeply on pioneer qualities. The qualities that saw neighbourly help as a spontaneous and unselfish act will have to be put on a larger global stage. Such a response would constitute a fitting tribute to the spirit upon which Calgary and indeed western Canada was built.

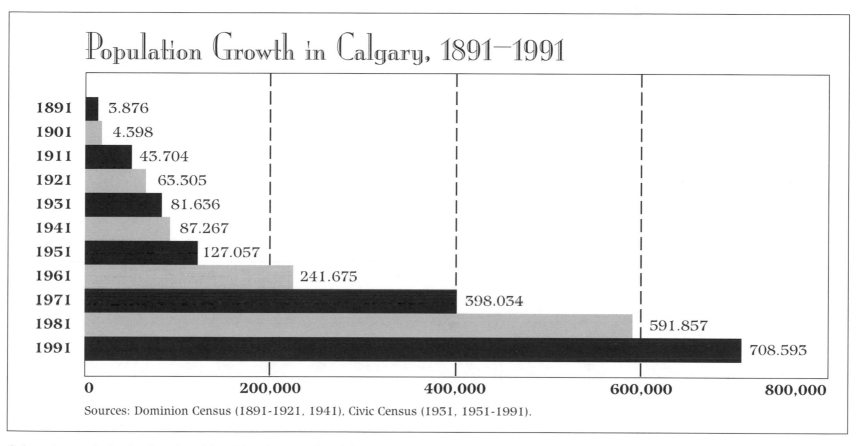

Population Growth in Calgary, 1891–1991

Year	Population
1891	3.876
1901	4.398
1911	43.704
1921	63.305
1931	81.636
1941	87.267
1951	127.057
1961	241.675
1971	398.034
1981	591.857
1991	708.593

0   200,000   400,000   600,000   800,000

Sources: Dominion Census (1891-1921, 1941), Civic Census (1931, 1951-1991).

Calgary's population by decade, 1891-1991. Sources: Dominion Census (1891-1921, 1941), Civic Census (1931, 1951-1991).

Calgary Timeline

Harry Sanders, City of Calgary Archives

Pre-1875 No permanent settlement. Aboriginal peoples camped seasonally in Calgary area, hunting in the river valley and finding winter shelter.

1875 North-West Mounted Police established Fort Calgary; I.G. Baker & Company and Hudson's Bay Company set up stores. Roman Catholic mission founded south of the fort, in present-day Mission district.

1877 Treaty Seven signed at Blackfoot Crossing with area Indians, creating conditions for non-Native settlement to take place.

1881 Cochrane Ranche established west of Calgary, heralding the emergence of ranching as the dominant regional industry.

1883 Canadian Pacific Railway arrived, linking Calgary with eastern centres; post office established; Calgary Herald began publishing.

1884 Calgary (population 400) incorporated as a town.

1885 Calgary School District #19 (predecessor to the Calgary Board of Education) created; first Protestant cemetery established on Dominion land at Shaganappi Point, today's Shaganappi Golf Course. (Owing to rocky soil, it was abandoned within seven years and replaced by Union Cemetery.)

1886 Calgary Tribune began publishing (in 1899 it is renamed the Albertan).

1887 Calgary Electric Lighting Company began supplying electric power. First telephones installed

1889 Calgary Water Power Company granted a contract for street lighting.

1890 Original Calgary General Hospital completed, replaced in 1895 by a substantial sandstone building. First phase of the town sewer system installed.

1892 Chinese community blamed for an outbreak of smallpox, and a small race riot ensued.

1893 Hull's Opera House (a 19th-century analogue to the Calgary Centre for Performing Arts) opened.

1894 Calgary, population 4,000, incorporated as a city. Wesley F. Orr elected as the city's first mayor.

1900 The city assumed the responsibility of supplying water when it purchased the waterworks operations of the Calgary Gas and Water Works Company.

1901 Annexation brought Victoria Park (now Stampede Park) within city limits.

1904 Named streets in downtown Calgary changed to numbered streets. Most names had been those of CPR officials.

1905 Province of Alberta created from the Northwest Territories; Calgary lost to Edmonton in its bid to become the provincial capital; the city inaugurated a municipally owned electric light plant.

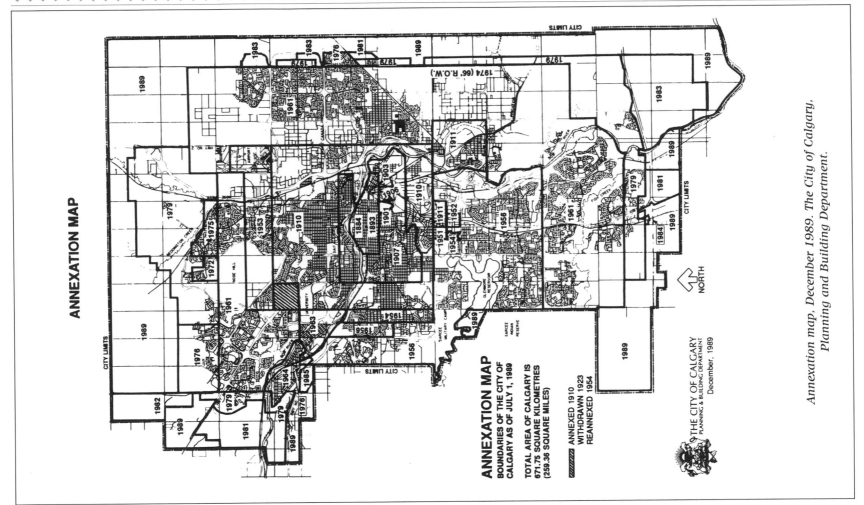

ANNEXATION MAP

ANNEXATION MAP

BOUNDARIES OF THE CITY OF CALGARY AS OF JULY 1, 1989

TOTAL AREA OF CALGARY IS 671.75 SQUARE KILOMETRES (259.36 SQUARE MILES)

ANNEXED 1910
WITHDRAWN 1923
REANNEXED 1954

THE CITY OF CALGARY
PLANNING & BUILDING DEPARTMENT
December, 1989

NORTH

Annexation map, December 1989. The City of Calgary, Planning and Building Department.

1906   Calgary Normal School, a teacher training college, began classes. This humble institution became the nucleus of the future University of Calgary.

1907   Calgary annexed Rouleauville (now Mission district), a largely francophone community south of town.

1908   The provincial government located the University of Alberta in Strathcona (now part of Edmonton) instead of Calgary; Calgary hosted the nation when the Dominion Exhibition was held at Victoria Park.

1909   The city-operated Calgary Municipal Railway began streetcar service.

1910   A growing Calgary annexed territory surrounding it on all sides, including its northern neighbour, the village of Crescent Heights.

1911   Calgary's population, at over 43,000, had increased tenfold in the ten years since 1901; Mount Royal College inaugurated as a Methodist institution.

1912   Calgary's apparently boundless prosperity culminated in 1912: the public library, funded in part by the Carnegie Foundation, opened its doors and also became home to a museum operated by the Calgary Natural History Society. (The museum closed its doors in 1926.) Calgary College, a privately endowed university, began classes at the library. (The provincial government refused to grant degree-conferring power, and the college closed in 1915.) Four wealthy ranchers, Pat Burns, A.E. Cross, George Lane, and A.J. McLean, known as the "Big Four," financed Guy Weadick's vision as a one-time event, and the Calgary Stampede was born. Natural gas from Bow Island piped to Calgary homes.

The faculty and student body of Calgary's first university on the steps of the Carnegie Public Library (now the Memorial Park Library), October 4, 1912, the first day of classes, Alexander Calhoun, the city librarian, appears in the front row on the extreme right. Glenbow Archives/NA-713-1.

1913   City Council commissioned Thomas Mawson, to develop a preliminary scheme for the future growth of Calgary. Mawson's report envisioned Calgary as a "Paris on the Prairies," but his elaborate scheme was only marginally implemented. The economic downturn and plummeting real estate prices signalled the end of Calgary's first great boom. Annie Graham Foote was elected as a trustee of the Calgary Public School Board. She became the first woman to serve on a civic committee.

1914 Oil was discovered at Turner Valley, and its proximity meant Calgary would become the centre of Alberta's oil industry. World War I began, ending in 1918; thousands enlisted in the city.

1916 Provincial Institute of Technology and Art (now the Southern Alberta Institute of Technology) inaugurated in Colonel Walker School. Classes in the permanent building on the North Hill began in 1922.

1917 Annie Gale, feminist and socialist, elected Alderman; she became the first woman in the British Empire elected to serve on a municipal council.

1918 Worldwide Spanish Influenza epidemic: public meetings banned in Calgary; face masks mandatory in public.

1919 The Calgary Stampede was revived as a one-time "Victory Stampede." The Prince of Wales (the future King Edward VIII) visited Calgary and purchased the nearby E.P. ranch.

1920 Victoria Park residents unsuccessfully petitioned City Council to remove blacks and make the area a whites-only district.

1921 First parking ticket issued.

1923 Calgary Exhibition and Stampede became an annual event.

1924 Calgary Tigers hockey club lost in the Stanley Cup playoffs to the Montreal Canadiens.

Father Doucet on a float, 1929. He first greeted the Mounties in 1874. Glenbow Archives/NA-2369-1.

1928 Calgary Public Museum opened its doors. Funded by the city, the provincial government and public subscriptions, this museum (heir to the defunct Calgary Natural History Society) operated until 1935, when funding evaporated. The collection was dispersed.

1929 Beginning of the decade-long Great Depression, in which many Calgarians joined the ranks of the unemployed. City relief and other charities fed thousands of jobless Calgary men, as well as others who "rode the rods" to town. Calgary Zoo opened. The "municipal flying field" in Renfrew became the Calgary Municipal Airport, and the Young Men's Section of the Calgary Board of Trade called on City Council to paint the name of Calgary, and arrows indicating the position of the landing field, on Calgary rooftops.

1930   Construction began on the Glenmore Dam, reservoir and water treatment plant, a municipal employment relief project. This 2 1/2-year project employed 1,000 Calgarians.

1931   Calgary Public Building, a federal government relief project, completed as the federal building.

1935   City aldermen received salaries for their services.

1936   Crude oil discovered at nearby Turner Valley, renewing Calgary's status as Canada's oil capital.

1939   Start of World War II, which ended in 1945. Calgary Municipal Airport changed its location to what became known in 1956 as McCall Field, named after Fred McCall, a World War I pilot, and the man credited with having brought aviation to the city. Calgary became a centre of the British Commonwealth Air Training Plan at Lincoln Park and the Technology Institute campus.

1945   Calgary Normal School became a branch of the University of Alberta Faculty of Education. As more faculties established Calgary branches, the city acquired the nucleus of the future University of Calgary.

1947   Oil discovered at Leduc, reviving the oil industry and cementing Calgary's position as the industry's administrative headquarters.

1948   Population exceeded 100,000; first parking meters installed; Calgary Stampeders football club first won the Grey Cup.

1950   Calgary Transit System, successor to the Calgary Municipal Railway, completed its conversion to trolley buses, and retired its last streetcar.

1955   Southern Alberta Jubilee Auditorium built.

1958   Population exceeded 200,000; sod turned for the present university campus, which was completed in 1960; Calgary Olympic Development Association (CODA) established, but its bids for the 1964 and 1968 Olympic Winter Games failed.

1961-
1964   Calgary annexed three satellite towns: Forest Lawn (incorporated in 1934, population 10,000), Montgomery (incorporated in 1958, population 5,000), and Bowness (incorporated in 1948, population 9,150).

1964   Heritage Park, a living-history village, opened to the public.

1966   University of Alberta, Calgary, became the autonomous University of Calgary.

1967   A $21 million urban renewal scheme for downtown was unveiled. In the next decade, scores of historic buildings were razed to make way for major projects such as the school board complexes, Glenbow Museum and Calgary Convention Centre, and bank and oil company towers; Husky Tower and Palliser Square (now Calgary Tower and Tower Centre) completed on the site of the old CPR station;

Centennial Planetarium completed at Mewata Park.
Bus fare set at twenty-five cents for adults.

1973-
1981   Rising oil prices led to another great boom pe-
        riod in Calgary, reminiscent of the pre-World
        War I years: rapid economic growth fostered
        sky-high expectations that were abruptly
        dashed.

1975   First leg of Deerfoot Trail, a major north-south
        freeway, opened to traffic.

1977   Original site of Fort Calgary, which had become
        a railway yard, rehabilitated as a centennial
        project; Fort Calgary Interpretive Centre opened.

1978   Population exceeded 500,000.

1980   The Albertan is purchased by the Toronto Sun
        Corporation and renamed The Calgary Sun.

1981   End of Calgary's great boom of the 1970s; first
        leg of LRT completed.

1985   Calgary Municipal Building and Calgary Cen-
        tre for Performing Arts opened.

1988   Calgary hosted the world with the XV Olympic
        Winter Games.

1989   In a "rematch" of the 1924 playoff, the Cal-
        gary Flames defeated the Montreal Canadiens
        and won the Stanley Cup.

1991   After five plebiscites over 34 years, the city fi-
        nally added fluoride to its water.

1994   Calgary celebrates its 100th birthday as a city.

The opening ceremonies for the 1988 Winter Olympics. Calgary Sun.

80

Calgary—A Select Bibliography

Prepared by Jennifer Bobrovitz, Marianne Fedori, Catherine Mayhood, and Maria Murray, Calgary Public Library, Local History

Alberta Historic Sites Service. *Driving Tour—Inglewood and Mount Royal, Calgary.* Edmonton: Alberta Culture, [1985].

At Your Service, Part One: Calgary's Library, Parks Department, Military, Medical Services, and Fire Department: Accounts. Century Calgary Historical Series 5. [Calgary]: Century Calgary Publications, 1975.

At Your Service, Part Two: Calgary's Police Force, Navy Base, Post Office, Transit System, and Private Service Groups. Century Calgary Historical Series 6. [Calgary]: Century Calgary Publications, 1975.

Bagnall, Lucy. *At the Sixtieth Milestone: The Story of the First Baptist Church, Calgary, Alberta 1888-1948.* Calgary: Jubilee Committee of the First Baptist Church, 1948.

Baine, Richard Paul. *Calgary: An Urban Study.* Toronto: Clarke, Irwin, 1973.

Baker, William M., ed. *Pioneer Policing—Southern Alberta: Deane of the Mounties 1888-1914.* Calgary: Historical Society of Alberta, 1993.

Barr, B.M., ed. *Calgary: Metropolitan Structure and Influence.* Western Geographical Series VII. Victoria: University of Victoria, 1975.

Barron, Sid. *Barron's Calgary Cartoons: 106 Cartoons From the Albertan.* [Calgary: The Albertan, 196?].

Baureiss, G.A. "The Chinese Community in Calgary." *Alberta Historical Review* no.2 (1974): 1-8.

Bedford, Judy. "Prostitution in Calgary, 1905-1914." *Alberta History* 29, no.2 (Spring 1981): 1-11.

Bedford, Judith B. "Social Justice in Calgary: A Study of Urban Poverty and Welfare Development in the 1920's." M.A. thesis, University of Calgary, 1981.

Belanger, Art, J. *Calgary-Edmonton, Edmonton-Calgary Trail.* Calgary: Frontier Pub. Ltd., 1973.

Birrell, Dave and Ron Ellis. *Calgary's Mountain Panorama.* Calgary, Rocky Mountain Books, 1990.

Bott, Robert. *University of Calgary, A Place of Vision.* Calgary: University of Calgary Press, 1990.

Boulet, Roger. *A.C. Leighton: A Retrospective Exhibition.* Edmonton: The Edmonton Art Gallery, 1981.

Bovey, Robin. *Birds of Calgary.* Rev. ed. Edmonton: Lone Pine Publishing, 1990.

Breen, David H. *Alberta's Petroleum Industry and the Conservation Board.* Edmonton: University of Alberta Press, 1993.

Breen, David, H. "Calgary: The City and the Petroleum Industry Since World War Two." *Urban History Review* 2-77 (October 1977): 55-77.

Breen, David H. *The Canadian Prairie West and the Ranching Frontier 1874-1924.* Toronto: University of Toronto Press, 1983.

Bullick, Terry. *Calgary Parks and Pathways.* Calgary: Rocky Mountain Books, 1991.

Bussard, Lawrence H. "Early History of Calgary." M.A. thesis, University of Alberta, 1935.

Byrne, M.B. Venini. *From the Buffalo to the Cross: A History of the Roman Catholic Diocese of Calgary.* Calgary: Calgary Archives and Historical Publishers, 1973.

Calgary. London; Toronto: Hodder and Stoughton, [1912].

Calgary Institute for the Humanities. *Calgary's Growth: Bane or Boon?* Calgary: The Calgary Institute for the Humanities, The University of Calgary, 1981.

Calgary 100: 100 Year History of Calgary. Calgary: Provost Promotions & Publications, 1974.

Calgary, the City Phenomenal. n.p.: 1912.

Calgary Zoological Society. "The First Fifty Years: The Calgary Zoo and Natural History Park—1929 to 1979." *Dinny's Digest* 4, no. 10 (Summer 1979).

Carter, David J. *Where the Wind Blows: A History of the Anglican Diocese of Calgary, 1888-1968*. [Calgary: Kyle Printing, 1968].

Central United Church (Calgary, Alta.). Centennial Book Committee. *They Gathered at the River*. Calgary: Central United Church, 1975.

Chestermere Historical Society. *Saddles, Sleighs and Sadirons*. [Calgary]: Chestermere Historical Society, 1971.

Communities of Calgary: From Scattered Towns to a Major City. Century Calgary Historical Series 3. [Calgary]: Century Calgary Publications, 1975.

Connery, Allan. *As Reported in the Herald*. Calgary: Calgary Herald, 1982.

Coppock, K. "Calgary and the Company." *Beaver* Outfit 271 (March 1941): 42-47.

Cunniffe, Richard. *Calgary in Sandstone*. [Calgary]: Historical Society of Alberta, Calgary Branch, 1969.

Daniels, Leroi A. "History of Education—Calgary." M.Ed. thesis, University of Washington, 1954.

Dempsey, Hugh A., ed. *The Best of Bob Edwards*. Edmonton: Hurtig, 1975.

Dempsey, Hugh A., ed. *The CPR West: The Iron Road and the Making of a Nation*. Vancouver: Douglas and McIntyre, 1984.

Dempsey, Hugh A., *Spirit of the West: A History of Calgary*. Saskatoon: Fifth House; Calgary: Glenbow, 1994.

Dempsey, Hugh A. *Indian Tribes of Alberta*. Rev. and upd. ed. Calgary: Glenbow Museum, 1986.

Donaldson, S.A. "William Pearce: His Vision of Trees." *Journal of Garden History* 3, no. 3 (July-September 1983): 233-244.

Dowbiggin, William F., ed. *Fire on Ice: The Flames*. 10th Anniversary ed. Edmonton: Executive Sport Publications, 1982.

Dyba, Ken. *Betty Mitchell*. Calgary: Detselig Press, 1986.

Edworthy Park Society. *Early Days in Edworthy Park and the Neighbouring Areas of Brickburn and Lowery Gardens*. Calgary: Edworthy Park Heritage Society. 1991.

Elphinstone, David. *Inglewood Bird Sanctuary: A Place For All Seasons*. Calgary: Rocky Mountain Books, 1990.

Elliott, David R. *Bible Bill: A Biography of William Aberhart*. Edmonton: Reidmore Books, 1987.

Elofson, Warren and John Feldberg, ed. *The Sarcee Elders*. Calgary: Consolidated Communications, 1990.

Farran, Roy. *History of the Calgary Highlanders, 1921-54*. [Calgary: Bryant Press, Ltd., 1955?].

Foothills Historical Society. *Chaps and Chinooks: A History West of Calgary*. 2 vols. [Calgary]: Foothills Historical Society, 1976.

Foran, Max. "Calgary Town Council, 1884-1895: A Study of Local Government—a Frontier Environment." M.A. thesis, University of Calgary, 1970.

Foran, Max. "Civic Corporation and Urban Growth: Calgary 1884-1930." Ph.D. thesis, University of Calgary, 1981.

Foran, M.L. "Early Calgary, 1875-1895: The Controversy Surrounding the Townsite Location and the Direction of Town Expansion." In *Cities in the West: Papers of the Western Canada Urban History Conference, University of Winnipeg, October 1974*, ed. A.R. McCormack and Ian MacPherson, 26-45. Ottawa: National Museum of Man, 1975.

Foran, M.L. "Land Development Patterns in Calgary, 1884-1945." *The Usable Urban Past: Planning and Politics in the Modern Canadian City*, ed. Alan F.J. Artibise and Gilbert A. Stelter, 293-315. Toronto: Macmillan, 1979.

Foran, Max. *Calgary: An Illustrated History*. Toronto: J. Lorimer; [Ottawa]: National Museum of Man, 1978.

Foran, Max. "Calgary, Calgarians and the Northern Movement of the Oil Frontier, 1950-70." In *The Making of the Modern West: Western Canada Since 1945*, ed. A.W. Rasporich, 115-132. Calgary: University of Calgary Press, 1984.

Foran, Max. *Calgary: Canada's Frontier Metropolis, An Illustrated History*. Burlington, Ontario: Windsor Publications, Inc., 1982.

Foran, Max. "Making of a Booster: Wesley Fletcher Orr and Nineteenth Century Calgary." In *Town and City: Aspects of Western Canadian Urban Development*, ed. Alan J. Artibise, 289-307. Regina: Canadian Plains Research Center, University of Regina, 1981.

Foran, Max, with Nonie Houlton. *Roland Gissing: The Peoples' Painter*. Calgary: University of Calgary Press, 1988.

Fraser, William B. *Calgary*. Toronto: Holt, Rinehart and Winston of Canada, 1967.

Galbraith, Judith. *Hey Kids! Discover Calgary: A Guide to Fun in the City*. Calgary: Galbraith Publishing, 1988.

Goodwin, Lou. *Fall Madness: A History of Senior and Professional Football in Calgary, 1908-1978*. [Calgary]: Calgary Stampeder Football Club, 1979.

Gowans, Bruce W. *Wings Over Calgary*. Calgary: Chinook County Chapter, Historical Society of Alberta, 1990.

Gray, James. *Talk to My Lawyer!: Great Stories of Southern Alberta's Bar & Bench*. Edmonton: Hurtig, 1987.

Gray, James H. *A Brand of Its Own: The 100 Year History of the Calgary Exhibition and Stampede*. Saskatoon: Western Producer Prairie Books, 1985.

Gray, James H. *R.B. Bennett: The Calgary Years*. Toronto: University of Toronto Press, 1991.

Guimond, Pierre S. *Calgary Architecture: The Boom Years, 1972-1982*. Calgary: Detselig Enterprises, 1984.

Hallworth, Beryl, ed. *Nose Hill: A Popular Guide*. Calgary: Calgary Field Naturalists Society, 1988.

Harasym, Donald G. "The Planning of New Residential Areas—Calgary, 1944-1973." M.A. thesis, University of Alberta, 1975.

Hatcher, Colin K. *Stampede City Streetcars: The Story of the Calgary Municipal Railway*. Montreal: Railfare Enterprises, 1975.

Hawkins, William. *Electrifying Calgary: A Century of Public & Private Power*. Calgary: University of Calgary Press, 1987.

Hiller, Harry H. "The Urban Transformation of a Landmark Event: The 1988 Calgary Winter Olympics". *Urban Affairs Quarterly* 26, no.1 (Sept. 1990):118-137.

House, J.D. *The Last of the Free Enterprisers: The Oilmen of Calgary.* Toronto: Macmillan of Canada; Ottawa: Institute of Canadian Studies, Carleton University, 1980.

Jackson, Christopher. *Marion Nicoll: Art and Influences.* Calgary: Glenbow Museum, 1986,

Jameson, Sheilagh S. *Chautauqua in Canada.* Calgary: Glenbow-Alberta Institute, 1979.

Jameson, Sheilagh S. and Max Foran, eds. *Citymakers: Calgarians after the Frontier.* [Calgary]: Chinook Country Chapter, Historical Society of Alberta, 1987.

Jenness, Diamond. *The Sarcee Indians of Alberta.* Ottawa: National Museum of Canada, 1938.

Jennings Publishing Company. *Merchants' and Manufacturers' Record: Calgary, Sunny Alberta, the Industrial Prodigy of the Great West.* Calgary: Jennings, 1911.

Joslin, Mark. *John Snow: Four Decades.* Edmonton: The Edmonton Art Gallery, 1990.

Kelly, L.V. *The Range Men.* Toronto: William Briggs, 1913.

Kennedy, Fred. *Calgary Stampede Story.* Calgary: T. Edwards Thonger, 1952.

Kerr, Illingworth. *Paint and Circumstance.* Calgary: J. and M. Poscente, 1987.

Klassen, Henry C. "Bicycles and Automobiles in Early Calgary." *Alberta History* 24, no.2 (1976): 1-8.

Klassen, Henry C. "I.G. Baker and Company—Calgary, 1875-1884." *Montana: the Magazine of Western History* 35 (Summer 1985): 40-55.

Klassen, Henry C. "Life in Frontier Calgary." In *Western Canada Past and Present*, ed. A.W. Rasporich, 42-57. Calgary: University of Calgary and McClelland and Stewart West, 1975.

Klassen, Henry C. "Social Troubles in Calgary in the Mid-1890's." *Urban History Review* 3-74 (February 1975): 8-16.

Klassen, N.J. "The Growth and Development of Music in Calgary, 1875-1920." M.A. thesis, University of Alberta, 1952.

Kwasny, Barbara and Elaine Peake. *A Second Look at Calgary's Public Art.* Calgary: Detselig Enterprises Ltd., 1992.

Lishman, Judith. *Alderman Mrs. Annie Gale.* Vancouver: S. Graham, 1985.

Lohnes, Donna and Barbara Nicholson. *Alexander Calhoun.* Calgary: Calgary Public Library, 1987.

Longair, Margaret E. *Development of Transportation in Early Calgary.* [Calgary]: Calgary Public School Board, 1968.

Lyon, Jim. *Dome: The Rise and Fall of the House That Jack Built.* Toronto: MacMillan of Canada, 1983.

MacDonald, R.H. *Grant MacEwan: No Ordinary Man.* Saskatoon: Western Producer Prairie Books, 1979.

MacEwan, Grant. *Calgary Cavalcade from Fort to Fortune.* New ed. Saskatoon: Western Producer Book Service, 1975.

MacEwan, Grant. *Colonel James Walker: Man of the Western Frontier.* Saskatoon: Prairie Books, 1989.

MacEwan, Grant. *Eye Opener Bob: The Story of Bob Edwards.* 2d ed. Saskatoon: Western Producer Book Service, 1974.

MacEwan, Grant. *He Left Them Laughing When He Said Good-Bye: The Life and Times of Frontier Lawyer Paddy Nolan.* Saskatoon: Western Producer Prairie Books, 1987.

MacEwan, Grant. *100 Years of Smoke, Sweat and Tears.* Calgary: Calgary Fire Department and Calgary Firefighters Association, 1984.

MacEwan, Grant. *Pat Burns: Cattle King.* Saskatoon: Western Producer Prairie Books, 1979.

Madiros, Anthony. *William Irvine: The Life of a Prairie Radical.* Toronto: J. Lorimer, 1979.

Mawson, Thomas H. *Calgary: A Preliminary Scheme for Controlling the Economic Growth of the City.* London: Thomas H. Mawson & Sons, [1914].

McDougall, Gerald M., ed. *Teachers of Medicine: The Development of Graduate Clinical Medical Education in Calgary.* Calgary: G.M. McDougall, 1987.

McGinnis, Janice D. and Frank Donnelly. *Reports on Selected Buildings in Calgary, Alberta.* Ottawa: Parks Canada, [1976].

McKee, Bill and Georgeen Klassen. *Trail of Iron: The CPR and the Birth of the West, 1880-1930.* [Calgary]: The Glenbow-Alberta Institute; Vancouver: Douglas & McIntyre, 1983.

McLennan, William M. *Bed and Breakfast: 'A History of Hostelries and Eating Establishments in the Area of Calgary.'* Calgary: Fort Brisebois Publishing, 1989.

McLennan, William M. *Entertainment in Early Calgary.* Calgary: Fort Brisebois Publishing, 1989.

McLennan, William M. *Sport in Early Calgary.* Calgary: Fort Brisebois Publishing, 1983.

McNeill, Leishman. *Calgary Herald's Tales of the Old Town.* Calgary: Calgary Herald, [1966].

Melnyk, Bryan P. *Calgary Builds: The Emergence of an Urban Landscape, 1905-1914.* [Edmonton]: Alberta Culture; Regina: Canadian Plains Research Center, 1985.

Melnyk, Brian. "Residential Buildings in Calgary, 1905-1914." *Prairie Forum* 8, no.1 (1983): 43-70.

Millar, Rob and Nancy Millar, comps. *A History of the Calgary Co-op.* Calgary: Calgary Co-operative Association, [1982].

Minhas, Manmohan Singh. *Sikh Society, Calgary—The First 25 Years.* Calgary: Sikh Society, Calgary, 1993.

Moore, Tom. *Sketches of Early Calgary.* [Calgary]: The Albertan, 1963.

Morning Albertan, Calgary, Alberta, Canada, 1914. [Calgary]: n.p., 1914.

Morrison, Elsie C. *Calgary, 1875-1950: A Souvenir of Calgary's Seventy-Fifth Anniversary.* Calgary: Calgary Publishing Co., [1950].

Morrow, E. Joyce. *"Calgary Many Years Hence": The Mawson Report in Perspective.* Calgary: City of Calgary and University of Calgary, 1979.

Mummery, Bob. *Countdown to the Stanley Cup: An Illustrated History of the Calgary Flames.* Winlaw, B.C.: Polestar Press, 1989.

Musselwhite, F.W. *Earle P. Scarlett: A Study in Scarlett.* Toronto: Hannah Institute and Dundurn Press, 1991.

Nodwell, Leila. *Calgary Guide: A Comprehensive Pocket Guide to Calgary's Attractions, Facilities and Services and Information on Points of Interest in the Surrounding Area Including Banff.* Calgary: Leila Nodwell, 1988.

Ogden Area History Committee. *Ogden Whistle: A History of Millican, Ogden Flats, Maryland, Valleyfield, Bonnybrook, South Hill, Cepeear, Lynwood, River Glen, Crestwood, C.P.R. Ogden Shops.* Calgary: Ogden Area History Committee, 1975.

Palmer, Harry. *Calgary Places and People*. Calgary: H. Palmer, 1983.

Palmer, Howard and Tamara Palmer. *Peoples of Alberta: Portraits of Cultural Diversity*. Saskatoon: Western Producer Prairie Books, 1985.

Past and Present: People, Places and Events in Calgary. Century Calgary Historical Series 1. [Calgary]: Century Calgary Publications, 1975.

Peach, Jack. *All Our Yesterdays*. Calgary: Calgary Herald, 1986.

Peach, Jack. *Days Gone By: Jack Peach on Calgary's Past*. Saskatoon: Fifth House, 1993.

Peach, Jack. *First Hundred Years: The History of the Calgary Chamber of Commerce*. Calgary: Calgary Chamber of Commerce, 1990.

Peach, Jack. *The First Fifty Years: A Chronicle of Half a Century in the Life of the Calgary Real Estate Board 1943-1993*. Calgary: Calgary Real Estate Board, 1993.

Peach, Jack. *In Sickness & In Health: Holy Cross Hospital: Celebrating Our First Century of Caring 1891-1991*. Calgary: Calgary District Hospital Group, 1991.

Peach, Jack. *100 Years of Connections, 1890-1990: The City of Calgary Sewer Division*. Calgary: City of Calgary, [1990].

Peach, Jack. *Partners: One Hundred Years of the Calgary Police Service*. Calgary: Canadian Trade and Industry Publishing Group, 1987.

Petrigo, Walter. *Petrigo's Calgary*. Calgary: W. Petrigo, 1987.

Philip, C.R. "The Women of Calgary and District, 1874-1914." M.A. thesis, University of Calgary, 1975.

Rasporich, A.W. and H.C. Klassen, eds. *Frontier Calgary: Town, City and Region, 1875-1914*. Calgary: University of Calgary and McClelland and Stewart West, 1975.

Reasons, Chuck, ed. *Stampede City: Power and Politics in the West*. Toronto: Between the Lines, 1984.

Robertson, Anna. *Guide to Fish Creek Provincial Park*. Calgary: Rocky Mountain Books, 1991.

Robertson, John H. "One Hundred Years Policing Calgary." *Fort Calgary Quarterly* 5, no.3 (Fall 1985) : 1-10.

Ryan, Joan. *Wall of Words. The Betrayal of the Urban Indian*. Toronto: Peter Martin Associates, 1978.

Ross, Charles W. *Calgary Knox, 1883-1983*. Calgary: n.p, 1983.

Sanders, Harry. "Hotels and Their Guests in Early Calgary." *Alberta History* 40, no.1 (Winter 1992): 3-7, 23-26.

Sanderson, Kay. "Vacant Lots Garden Club, 1914-1951." *Fort Calgary Quarterly* 6, no.3 (Summer 1986): 13-16.

Scollard, D. *Hospital: A Portrait of Calgary General*. Calgary: Calgary General Hospital, 1981.

Search for Souls: Histories of Calgary Churches: Accounts. Century Calgary Historical Series 4. [Calgary]: Century Calgary Publications, 1975.

Sherrington, Peter, ed. *Calgary's Natural Areas: A Popular Guide*. Calgary: Calgary Field Naturalists' Society, 1975.

Shiels, Bob. *Calgary*. Calgary: Calgary Herald, 1974.

Simon, Maurice. *Community With a View: A Heritage Tour of Bridgeland-Riverside*. Calgary: Bridgeland Riverside Community Association, 1989.

Snow, Kathleen M. *Maxwell Bates, Biography of an Artist*. Calgary: University of Calgary Press, 1993.

Soby, Trudy. *A Walk Through Old Calgary*. Century Calgary Historical Series. [Calgary]: Century Calgary Publications, 1975.

Soby, Trudy. *Be It Every So Humble*. Century Calgary Historical Series. [Calgary]: Century Publications, 1975.

Soby, Trudy. *Fort Calgary*. Calgary: City of Calgary, 1978.

Sparks, Susie, ed. *Calgary: A Living Heritage*. Calgary: Junior League of Calgary, 1984.

Stamp, Robert M. *School Days: A Century of Memories*. Calgary: Calgary Board of Education and McClelland and Stewart West, 1975.

Stenson, Fred. *The Story of Calgary: An Illustrated Short History*. Saskatoon: Fifth House Publishers, 1994.

Stuart, E. Ross. *The History of Prairie Theatre: The Development of Theatre—Alberta, Manitoba and Saskatchewan 1833-1982*. Toronto: Simon and Pierre Publishing Co. Ltd., 1984.

Thomas, Lewis G. "The Rancher and the City: Calgary and the Cattlemen, 1883-1914." *Royal Society of Canada. Transactions* 4th ser., 6 (1968): 203-215.

Thorner, Thomas. "Not So Peaceable Kingdom: A Study of Crime in Southern Alberta." M.A. thesis, University of Alberta, 1976.

Treacy, Robert M. *Sandstone, Brick and Wood: A Collection of Calgary Pioneer Homes and Histories*. [Calgary]: n.p., 1975.

United Calgary Chinese Association. *A Century of the Chinese in Calgary*. Calgary: United Chinese Association, 1993.

Utas, Gregory P. "Calgary Architecture, 1875-1915." M.E. Des. thesis, Calgary: University of Calgary, 1976.

Ward, Tom. *Cowtown: An Album of Early Calgary*. [Calgary]: City of Calgary Electric System and McClelland and Stewart West, 1975.

Watson, Neil B. "Calgary: A Study of Crime, Offenders and the Police Court, 1929-1934." M.A. thesis, University of Calgary, 1979.

Weisenburger, William, ed. *Milestones & Mementoes, 1885-1985: A Century of Firefighting*. Calgary: Calgary Fire Department, 1985.

Welin, R.A. *Bridges of Calgary, 1882-1977*. Calgary: City of Calgary, Engineering Department, 1977.

West Hillhurst Go-Getters (Calgary, Alta.), compl. *Harvest of Memories: Grand Trunk, West Hillhurst, Calgary*. Calgary: West Hillhurst Go-Getters, 1987.

Wetherell, Donald G. *Useful Pleasures: The Shaping of Leisure in Alberta, 1896-1945*. [Edmonton]: Alberta Culture and Multiculturalism; Regina: Canadian Plains Research Centre, University of Regina, 1990.

Williams, Vicky. *Calgary, Then and Now*. Vancouver: Bodima Books, 1978.

Wilkin, Karen. *Painting in Alberta. An Historical Survey*. Edmonton: The Edmonton Art Gallery, 1980.

Wilson, Michael C. and Kenneth J. Hardy. "The Archaeology of the Calgary Area, Alberta." In *Geology of the Calgary Area*, ed. L.E. Jackson and M.C. Wilson. Calgary: Canadian Society of Petroleum Geologists, 1987.

Wright, Bruce W. "The Archaeology of Fort Calgary." *Fort Calgary Quarterly* 2, no.3 (Summer 1982): 1-6.

Young People of All Ages: Sports, Schools and Youth Groups in Calgary. Century Calgary Historical Series 3. [Calgary]: Century Calgary Publications, 1975.

Fiction

Adam, Ian. *Glass Canyons*. Edmonton: NeWest Press, 1985.

Ballem, John. *The Barons*. Hanna, Alta.: Gorman and Gorman Ltd, 1991.

Eggleston, Wilfred. *Prairie Symphony*. Ottawa: Borealis Press, 1978.

Govier, Katherine. *Between Men*. Markham, Ont.: Viking, 1987.

Harker, Herbert. *Goldenrod*. New York: Random House, 1972.

Mitchell, W.O. *For Art's Sake.* Toronto: McClelland and Stewart, 1992.

Ravvin, Norman. *Cafe des Westens.* Red Deer, Alta.: Red Deer College, 1991.

Wiebe, Rudy. *My Lovely Enemy.* Toronto: McClelland and Stewart, 1983.

Wright, L.R. *Among Friends.* Toronto: Doubleday, 1984.